Corporatocracy

YOU ARE A
CORPORATE CITIZEN

A SLAVE OF INVISIBLE
AND RUTHLESS MASTERS

By
Dr. Sahadeva dasa

B.com., FCA., AICWA., PhD
Chartered Accountant

Soul Science University Press

www.souleconomics.org

1

Readers interested in the subject matter of this
book are invited to correspond with the publisher at:
SoulScienceUniversity@gmail.com   +91 98490 95990
or visit DrDasa.com

First Edition: January 2015

Soul Science University Press expresses its gratitude to the
Bhaktivedanta Book Trust International (BBT), for the use of quotes by
His Divine Grace A.C.Bhaktivedanta Swami Prabhupada.

ISBN 978-93-82947-20-2

Published by:
Dr. Sahadeva dasa for Soul Science University Press

Printed by:
Rainbow Print Pack, Hyderabad

To order a copy write to purnabramhadasa@gmail.com
or buy online: Amazon.com, rlbdeshop.com

Dedicated to....

His Divine Grace A.C.Bhaktivedanta Swami Prabhupada

Unfortunately, these leaders, actually they do not want people should be very intelligent. You see? They want to keep the people in ignorance and exploit their ignorance for their personal benefits. That is their policy. Actually they do not want welfare of the citizens. They want only the post, and bluffing the citizens they want to get votes.

That is their policy, all these politicians. They have no thinking how people will be happy. That is beyond their dreaming, neither they want it.

But actually these position—this mayor or governor or topmost head—they should be thinking of the welfare of the people. But it is just the opposite.

Instead of thinking of their welfare: they are thinking how to exploit them and make their position secure.

They are politicians. They are not interested that people should go back to home, back to Godhead. They are interested that they must remain foolish and pay taxes and enjoy, that's all. That is their position. All bad character rascals, cheaters. That is my opinion. Cheaters number one. They have no good wishes for the people in their hearts. They don't want that people should become advanced in philosophy, in religion, in character. No. They don't want. They want to keep them in darkness.

~ Srila Prabhupada (Conversation, Los Angeles)

By The Same Author

Oil–Final Countdown To A Global Crisis And Its Solutions
End of Modern Civilization And Alternative Future
To Kill Cow Means To End Human Civilization
Cow And Humanity - Made For Each Other
Cows Are Cool - Love 'Em!
Let's Be Friends - A Curious, Calm Cow
Wondrous Glories of Vraja
We Feel Just Like You Do
Tsunami Of Diseases Headed Our Way - Know Your Food Before Time Runs Out
Cow Killing And Beef Export - The Master Plan To Turn India Into A Desert
Capitalism Communism And Cowism - A New Economics For The 21st Century
Noble Cow - Munching Grass, Looking Curious And Just Hanging Around
World - Through The Eyes Of Scriptures
To Save Time Is To Lengthen Life
Life Is Nothing But Time - Time Is Life, Life Is Time
Lost Time Is Never Found Again
Spare Us Some Carcasses - An Appeal From The Vultures
An Inch of Time Can Not Be Bought With A Mile of Gold
Cow Dung For Food Security And Survival of Human Race
Cow Dung – A Down To Earth Solution To Global Warming And Climate Change
Career Women - The Violence of Modern Jobs And The Lost Art of Home Making
Working Moms And Rise of A Lost Generation
Glories of Thy Wondrous Name
India A World Leader in Cow Killing And Beef Export - An Italian Did It In 10 Years
As Long As There Are Slaughterhouses, There Will Be Wars
Peak Soil – Industrial Civilization, On The Verge of Eating Itself
If Violence Must Stop, Slaughterhouses Must Close Down
(More information on availability on DrDasa.com)

Contents

Preface

A government is the system by which a state or community is governed. This usage is analogous to what is called an 'administration'. A form of government refers to the set of political systems and institutions that make up the organisation of a specific government.

Government of any kind affects every human activity in many important ways. For this reason, political scientists generally argue that government should not be studied by itself; but should be studied along with anthropology, economics, history, philosophy, and sociology.

Over the centuries, the world has seen different types of governments. The Classical Greek philosopher Plato discusses five types of regimes - aristocracy, timocracy, oligarchy, democracy and tyranny. These five regimes progressively degenerate starting with aristocracy at the top and tyranny at the bottom.

Then there are many other forms of government like monarchy, geniocracy, kratocracy, meritocracy, autocracy, dictatorship, fascism, diarchy, nepotocracy, kleptocracy, ochlocracy, netocracy, theocracy, stratocracy, plutocracy, maoism, anocracy, anarchy, bureaucracy, feudalism, magocracy and technocracy.

History has witnessed each of these regimes at one point in time or the other.

But today the world is ruled by one homogenous system of government called corporatocracy. Today irrespective of the country you live in, you are living under the rule of big business corporations. No matter who your president is, business corporations run your government. They control or greatly influence what you eat and drink, where you live, what you wear and even what you're taught in schools up to the highest levels. Through advertising, public relations, and mass media, they shape your views of the world and your views of each other.

They even now own patents on our genetic code, the most basic elements of human life, and are likely planning to manipulate and control them as just another commodity to exploit for profit. Corporations stand as the dominant institutions in our society. They provide the products and services upon which most of us have come to depend.

In this greed-propelled growth of human society, this institution stands tall over others, working silently in the background, casting its dark shadows all over. Parliaments are only meant to endorse what is already decided in the boardrooms.

It's high time you got acquainted with your invisible masters.

Sahadeva dasa

Dr. Sahadeva dasa
1st January 2015
Secunderabad, India

Man Today Is As Much A Slave

As He Was In Any Other Time

Since time immemorial, various institutions have exerted control over human society. At times it was the monarchy, at other times it was the church and yet another time, it was the communist party. These institutions governed the social order and the behavior of a set of individuals within a given human community. Institutions were identified with a social purpose and permanence, transcending individual human lives and intentions, and with the making and enforcing of rules governing cooperative human behavior.

The human society has never been able to free itself from the institutional control. Even speaking of our personal lives, we are controlled at every moment. We are controlled by our senses, which oblige us to eat, sleep, defend and engage in sex, and we are controlled by the natural laws of birth, old age, disease and death. No one wants to become old or diseased, but old age and disease are thrust upon us. No one wants to die, but everyone must.

> *"Those who manipulate the organized habits and opinions of the masses constitute an invisible government which is the true ruling power of our country."*
> *~ Edward Bernays*

In a civilized and free world, an exuberant citizen can take solace at all the rights and liberties available to him today. He can look down with disdain at the civilization's 'dark' past. With all the amenities at his disposal, he has the right to celebrate his birth in these times.

But these are the times when more blood is spilling than any other time in the history. Communication revolution has expanded the war zones to include the whole world. 20th century has been the bloodiest century in human history. This century witnessed, besides the two most brutal World Wars, the worst acts of barbarism — holocaust, Gulag Concentration camps, genocides and atomic bombing of Hiroshima and Nagasaki.

These are the times when every year, the world is losing 24 billion tons of top soil, 44 million acres of forests are getting destroyed, 15 million acres of new deserts are forming and massive quantities of carbon-dioxide being pumped into the atmosphere, over-heating the earth and transforming it into a virtual pressure-cooker.

And further, in these times, we have given birth to a global set-up where disparities in incomes is widening, where 20 per cent of people have cornered 86 per cent of the world's gross product, and where the bottom 80 per cent live on $1 a day.

The progress of human society has carried the cancerous seeds of its own destruction. In this greed-propelled growth of human society, one institution stands tall over others, working silently in the background, casting its dark shadows all along - and that is a 'corporation'.

Like the church, monarchy or the communist party in former times, the corporation is today's dominant institution, and it

In the modern civilized world, everyone is proud to be free and independent but a closer look at the facts would prove it otherwise. Man today is as much a slave as he was in any other time in the past history. All the claims of independence and freedom in reality are not as tenable as they are advertised to be.

~ Steve Hopkins

manipulates and controls almost every aspect of our lives. What started off as a small legal enterprise designed to harness human ingenuity and entrepreneurship for the public good has been transformed into a largely unaccountable force that has, in some instances, grown larger than entire nations.

A Dark History Of Greed And Deception

History of corporations is a history of greed, exploitation and plunder. During the time of colonial expansion in the 17th century, the true progenitors of the modern corporation emerged as the "chartered company".

Many European nations chartered these companies to lead colonial ventures and these companies came to play a large part in the history of colonialism and mercantilism. These companies were instrumental in maintaining draconian control over trade, resources and territory in Asia, Africa, and the Americas.

In 1601 Queen Elizabeth I created the East India Trading Company. Labeled by both contemporaries and historians as "the grandest society of merchants in the universe", the British East India Company would come to symbolize the dazzlingly rich potential of the corporation, as well as new methods of business that could be both brutal and exploitive.

It shipped out gold and silver to Asia in return for spices, textiles and luxury goods. The East India Company expanded into a vast enterprise, conquering India with a total monopoly on trade and all the territorial powers of a government. At its height, it ruled over a fifth of the world's population with a private army of a quarter of a million.

Britain had fiercely protected its own textile industry and forced the Indian market open. In the words of Governor-General William Bendick, 'The bones of the cotton weavers are bleaching the plains of India'. Conditions under the colonial capitalists led to the Rebellion ('Mutiny') of 1857. In 1858 Britain reined in the East India Company, dissolving its territorial power and making India the responsibility of the British crown. The Company continued trading opium to China, which led to the Opium Wars of the 19th century.

As early as 1611, shareholders in the East India Company were earning an almost 150% return on their investment. Subsequent stock offerings demonstrated just how lucrative the Company had become.

As England sought to build a mercantile Empire, the government created corporations under a Royal Charter or an Act of Parliament with the grant of a monopoly over a specified territory. Corporations at this time would essentially act on the government's behalf, bringing in revenue from its exploits abroad.

A similar chartered company, the South Sea Company, was established in 1711 to trade in the Spanish South American colonies, but met with less success. The South Sea Company's monopoly rights were supposedly backed by a treaty, signed in 1713 as a settlement following the War of Spanish Succession, which gave the United Kingdom rights to trade in the region for thirty years. In fact the Spanish remained hostile and let only one ship a year enter. Unaware of the problems, investors in the UK, enticed by extravagant promises of profit from company promoters bought thousands of shares. By 1717, the South Sea Company was so wealthy (still having done no real business) that it assumed the public debt of the UK government. This accelerated the inflation of the share price further. The share price rose so rapidly that people began buying shares merely in order to sell them at a higher price, which in turn led to higher share prices. This was the first speculative bubble the country had seen, but by the end of 1720, the bubble had "burst", and the share price sank from £1000 to under £100. This resulted in many bankruptcies and the mood against corporations, and errant directors, was bitter.

Then there was Dutch East India Company (VOC), Acting under a charter sanctioned by the Dutch monarch. It defeated Portuguese forces and established itself in the Moluccan Islands in order to profit from the European demand for spices.

Investors in the company were issued paper certificates as proof of share ownership, and were able to trade their shares on the original Amsterdam stock exchange. Shareholders are also explicitly granted limited liability in the company's royal charter.

In the late 18th century, Stewart Kyd, the author of the first treatise on corporate law in English, defined a corporation as:

"A collection of many individuals united into one body, under a special denomination, having perpetual succession under an artificial form, and vested, by policy of the law, with the capacity of acting, in several respects, as an individual, particularly of taking and granting property, of contracting obligations, and of suing and being sued, of enjoying privileges and immunities in common, and of exercising a variety of political rights, more or less extensive, according to the design of its institution, or the powers conferred upon it, either at the time of its creation, or at any subsequent period of its existence." (A Treatise on the Law of Corporations)

At The Dawn of The Industrial Age

The turning point came with the dawn of the industrial age. That's when the concept of corporate enterprise really took off. It grew out of the industrial age and it, in its turn, fueled the growth of the industrial age.

Industrial age began when some one in Europe invented a steam driven pump to pump water out of the coalmines, so the coalminers could get more coal out of the mine.

It was all about productivity, more coal per man-hour. That was the dawn of the industrial age. And then it became more steel per man hour, more textiles per man hour, more automobiles per man hour.

But industrial production had to be marketed and the colonies became a captive market. Like in Asia and Africa, in America also corporations ran their colonies with ruthless monopoly powers and resentment was brewing against the British rule. Royal charters decreed that raw material was shipped from the colonies to Britain for manufacture, with the colonies forced to purchase the finished goods.

Taking Root In America

The American Revolutionary War began in 1776 with a determination to rout the British. Adam Smith, the father of free-trade theories, who published Wealth of Nations in the same year as the Declaration of Independence (1776), argued that large business associations limit competition: 'The pretence that corporations are necessary to the better government of the trade is without foundation.'

After Independence, America's founders retained a healthy fear of corporate power and wisely limited corporations exclusively to a business role. Corporations were forbidden from attempting to influence elections, public policy, and other realms of civic society.

Initially, the privilege of incorporation was granted selectively to enable activities that benefited the public, such as construction of

Corporations were conceived and first chartered to serve the public good — to exploit hard-to-find resources and to undertake projects individual businesspeople couldn't manage alone. But times have changed, corporate executives have taken on regal authority, and the public good has been dropped from the equation.

Modern corporations are free to maximize their wealth but owe nothing to the individuals and communities around them. They balk at government regulation and lock out shareholders while executives use inside baseball to reward themselves with massive pay packages. Today's CEOs are beholden to one thing only—profit for profit's sake—and our communities, our workforce, and our environment frequently suffer for it. While over-regulation of corporations will destroy the economy, doing nothing to change corporate behavior might well destroy everything else.

Shareholder control over large corporations is as weak as it has ever been. Not only are corporations rarely held to account by government regulation, they face even less control by those whose interests they ostensibly serve.

~ Robert A. G. Monks

roads or canals. Their charters lasted between 10 and 40 years, often requiring the termination of the corporation on completion of a specific task. Enabling shareholders to profit was seen as a means to that end. For 100 years after the American revolution, legislators maintained tight control of the corporate chartering process.

In Europe, charters protected directors and stockholders from liability for debts and harms caused by their corporations. American legislators explicitly rejected this corporate shield. The penalty for abuse or misuse of the charter was not a plea bargain and a fine, but dissolution of the corporation.

Slowly, though, corporations were gaining power. In 1819, the Supreme Court ruled in a landmark case that states could not alter a contract granted by a previous legislature and thus creating a framework of protection for corporations against government encroachment.

As industrialization began reshaping America, great fortunes began accumulating in the hands of canal owners and financiers and later railroad and steel magnates. And as great fortunes accumulated, a new wealthy class began influencing policymaking, changing the rules governing the corporations they owned. Charters grew longer and less restrictive. The doctrine of limited liability – allowing corporate owners and managers to avoid responsibility for harm and losses caused by the corporation began to appear in state corporate laws.

Transition - From The Era Of Self-Sufficiency To The Era Of Corporate Market Dominance

The growing industrialization of America in the second half of the 19th century meant more citizens were leaving the countryside farms for work in the cities. A wave of immigration swelled the ranks of the urban workers, creating a new class that depended on factory jobs to earn a living and depended on factory products to survive. The era of self-sufficiency was ending and the era of corporate market dominance was beginning.

The industrial age forced a nation of farmers to become wage earners, and they became fearful of unemployment--a new fear that corporations quickly learned to exploit. Company towns arose. and blacklists of labor organizers and workers who spoke up for their rights became common. When workers began to organize, industrialists and bankers hired private armies to keep them in line. They bought newspapers to paint businessmen as heroes and shape public opinion.

Meanwhile, corporations were expanding their power through both courts and legislatures, both of which were increasingly packed with sympathizers. In 1886, corporations emerged from a Supreme Court case as "persons" under the law and thus could use the 14th Amendment (enacted to protect rights of freed slaves) to protect their equal rights. This meant that corporations were now entitled to free speech, protection from searches and seizures, and could not be discriminated against. Suddenly, corporations (artificial persons) had the same rights as real people. Armed with these "rights," corporations increased control over resources, jobs, commerce, politicians, even judges and the law.

If aliens came
and poisoned half our rivers
and wiped out 1 wild species in 10
and dismantled entire mountains
and laced agricultural lands with poisons
and put cancerous materials into children's toys
and torched and hacked down our forests
and radically changed our atmosphere

Would we get the supreme court to declare them persons
and give them all our money?
Or would we mobilize to stop them?

Meanwhile, between 1895 and 1904, the first great merger wave consolidated 1,800 companies into 137 mega corporations or "trusts." When all was said and done, the corporation was transformed from a quasi-public, state-controlled organization limited in size to a gigantic unlimited private organization with limited responsibility and limited accountability.

Corporatocracy

maximize profits, regardless of the social and environmental cost

Meanwhile, as corporations grew larger and larger and more and more people began to own stock, a new problem emerged – the owners (now an increasingly diffuse network of individual investors) no longer controlled the corporation. Instead, managers were running the company at their whims, accountable to no one. Now, with ownership increasingly divorced from management, owners took little interest in how their company was being run and managers had few consequences for mismanagement.

Educated Slaves

The modern education means to create dogs. The dog goes door to door and moves the tail, "Please give me if you have anything." So this educated person with application goes, and they say, "No vacancy. Get out." Educated means dogs. They are creating dogs. Then again he wags his tail, goes to another place.

What is the use? The big, big technologists, unless they get a suitable job, they're just like dog. Dog is loitering in the street, no food. So these men with all this high technological knowledge, if they do not get a proper master, their degrees are completely useless.

~ Srila Prabhupada (Room Conversation -- January 26, 1977, Puri)

This meant that managers could more easily use the corporations to enrich themselves at the expense of workers or employees, as they increasingly did.

America emerged from World War II as the dominant global power and the world's major exporter.

This helped U.S. corporations to become increasingly wealthy. Today, the power of transnational corporations is greater than that of many nation-states. However, now as then, social movements and resistance to unrestrained global capitalism are also growing, questioning the legitimacy of corporate rule.

Reference

Sobel, Robert. The Age of Giant Corporations: a Microeconomic History of American Business. (1984)

Ebert, Robert (July 16, 2004). "The Corporation, review". Chicago Sun-Times.

The lunatic you work for, review in The Economist, May 6, 2004

Snakes in Suits: When Psychopaths Go to Work. HarperCollins. 2007

2

Corporation

Defined

Ambrose Bierce's Devil's Dictionary defines a corporation as 'an ingenious device for obtaining profit without individual responsibility'. It is a legal construct, a charter granted by the state to a group of investors to gather private funds for a specific purpose. Originally, charters were granted in the service of a public purpose, and could be revoked if this were not fulfilled.

The relationship between state and corporation is a complex one. Over the past 400 years corporations have conquered territory and brought in resources for the state, breaking laws put in place to constrain them and gaining in power and privilege. History shows a repetitive cycle of corporations over-reaching, causing such social turmoil that the state is forced to reign them back in through regulation.

The word 'corporation' derives from 'corpus', the Latin word for body, or a 'body of people'. Thus a corporation is a legal entity that is created under the laws of a state designed to establish the entity as a separate legal entity having its own privileges and liabilities distinct from those of its members. There are many different forms of corporations, most of which are used to conduct business. Early corporations were established by charter and many of these chartered companies still exist. Most jurisdictions now allow the creation of a new corporation through registration.

Corporations exist strictly as a product of the corporate law. An important (but not universal) contemporary feature of a corporation is limited liability. If a corporation fails, shareholders normally only stand to lose their investment and employees will lose their jobs, but neither will be further liable for debts that remain owing to the corporation's creditors.

Despite not being natural persons, corporations are recognized by the law to have rights and responsibilities like natural persons ("people"). Corporations can exercise human rights against real individuals and the state, and they can themselves be responsible for human rights violations. Corporations are conceptually immortal but they can "die" when they are "dissolved" either by statutory operation, order of court, or voluntary action on the part of shareholders. Insolvency may result in a form of corporate 'death', when creditors force the liquidation and dissolution of the corporation under court order, but it most often results in a restructuring of corporate holdings. Corporations can even be convicted of criminal offenses, such as fraud and manslaughter.

Although corporate law varies in different jurisdictions, there are four core characteristics of the business corporation:
-Legal personality
-Limited liability
-Transferable shares
-Centralized management under a board structure

Companies start life with a birth certificate--incorporation. Growing up, they can fool around--Yahoo and Facebook are swapping corporate fluids right now. They can marry--a Comcast

Greed, cruelty, the will to control and own, these are basic human qualities that take on a much larger role in corporation-dominated cultures, simply because the corporation greatly extends human power to carry them out.
~ Jennifer Smith

and NBC wedding is in the air. They can divorce--as Time Warner and AOL recently did. And they can have children like Virgin or adopt them like Diageo.

A company can violate human rights and be tried for fraud and manslaughter. In lots of ways a company is just like any of us, but with one big exception. As long as it turns a profit, it's immortal.

Reference

Drucker, P.F. 1946, Concept of the corporation, The John Day Company, New York.

Forsgren, M. 2013, Theories of the multinational firm: A multidimensional creature in the global economy, Edward Elgar Publishing.

Corporation - A Private Government

A Power Unto Itself

Something New In Civilization

Major public corporations have evolved into something new in civilization, structures more massive, more dominant in the world than our democratic forefathers dreamed possible. They left us little guidance on governing these institutions – the word "corporation" appears nowhere in any Constitution – because only a handful of American corporations existed when that seminal document was written in America.

They are causing increasing damage to our ecosystem. The rules of accounting were written in the sixteenth century, when nature seemed an unlimited reservoir of resources, and an unlimited sink for wastes. That is no longer true, but

"**Corporations** are Not concerned with the Common Good. They Exploit, Pollute, Impoverish, Repress, Kill and Lie to make money. They throw poor People out of Homes, let the Uninsured Die, wage useless Wars for Profit, Poison and Pollute the Ecosystem, slash Social Assistance programs, gut public Education, trash the Global Economy, plunder the U.S. treasury and crush all popular movements that seek justice for working men and women. They worship Money and Power."

— Chris Hedges
in 'The Death of the Liberal Class'

the rules of accounting retain fossilized remnants of those ancient attitudes.

Washington and Jefferson governed a nation of farmers, in which most nonagricultural businesses were indeed "private," run out of the parlor, or in the barn, as part of the private household.

As the name itself implies, "public" corporations are no longer private. The major corporation, as Franklin D. Roosevelt observed, "represents private enterprise become a kind of private government which is a power unto itself."

The Corporate Control

Of Human Civilization

Corporations stand as the dominant institutions in our society. They provide the products and services upon which most of us have come to depend. Through advertising, public relations, and mass media, they shape our views of the world and our views of each other.

They handle our finances and our health care, even our ability to communicate with each other. They provide most of our jobs. They wield more influence over the legislative process than any government branch was ever supposed to wield. They increasingly provide many essential services, including water, electricity, and health care. Even public schools, universities, and churches have turned to corporations for funding, opening up once sacred spaces to commercialization. Meanwhile most natural countervailing force against corporate power, organized labor, has become increasingly powerless.

Finance Is The Key

In our world, finance has a hold on almost every single part of our lives – from the day we're born, until we take our last breath. Capitalism and the quest for larger profits have taken hold of our healthcare, our education, our homes, our communication, and even our government. Today, most babies are born in for-profit hospitals, and their medical claims are paid by for-profit insurance. As children grow, many go to for-profit charter schools or private schools, and our public education system continues to crumble. Young adults are forced to deal with for-profit lenders to go to college at for-profit universities, and everything from their backpack to their first home will generate a profit for someone on Wall Street.[1]

Throughout our lives, we are forced into paying huge monopolies for access to phones and internet and communication, and all that data is turned over to for-profit corporations who spy on us for our government. Even the vast majority of our elected leaders answer first to corporate lobbyists, and second to the general public. Corporate power has a stranglehold on our entire existence, and it has turned our entire lives into a profit-making venture.[2]

They're preeminent throughout the world but especially in the Global North and its epicenter in the US. They control or greatly influence what we eat and drink, where we live, what we wear and even what we're taught in schools up to the highest levels. They even now own patents on our genetic code, the most basic elements of human life, and are likely planning to manipulate and control them as just another commodity to exploit for profit in their brave new world that should concern everyone.

They also carefully craft their image and use catchy slogans to convince us of their benefit to society and the world, like: "better things for better living through chemistry" (if you don't mind toxic air, water and soil), "we bring good things to life" for them, not us), and "all the news that's fit to print" (only if you love state and corporate friendly disinformation and propaganda). The slogans are clever, but the truth is ugly.

According to The Company by John Micklethwait and Adrian Wooldridge, in 2000 there were 5.5 million corporations in the U.S., and zero in North Korea.

Corporations Decide Who Will Govern Us

Government, Military And All Other Institutions Serve Their Interests

Corporations also decide who will govern and how. We may think we do, but it's not so and never was. Those national elections only look legitimate to most people, but not to those who know and understand how the system works. Here's how it really works.

The "power elite" or "privileged class" Charles Wright Mills wrote about 50 years ago in his classic book by that title are the real king and decision makers. He wrote how corporate, government and military elites formed a trinity of power after WW II and that

the "power elite" were those "who decide whatever is decided" of importance.

The holy trinity Mills wrote about still exists but today in the shape of a triangle with the transnational giants clearly on top and government, the military and all other institutions of importance there to serve their interests. These corporations have become so large and dominant they run our lives and the world, and in a zero

---

The bottom line is that the government is getting what they ordered. They do not want your children to be educated. They do not want you to think too much. That is why our country and our world has become so proliferated with entertainments, mass media, television shows, amusement parks, drugs, alcohol, and every kind of entertainment to keep the human mind entertained so that you don't get in the way of important people by doing too much thinking. You better wake up and understand that there are people who are guiding your life and you don't even know it.

~ Jordan Maxwell:

sum world and the chips that count most in their stack, they do it for their continuing gain and at our increasing expense.

The Power Of Transnational Corporations And The Harm They Cause

As corporations have grown in size they've gained in power and influence. And so has the harm they cause - to communities, nations, the great majority of the public and the planet. Today corporate giants decide who governs and how, who serves on our courts, what laws are enacted and even whether and when wars are fought, against whom and for what purpose or gain. It's for their gain, who else's, certainly not ours. Once we start one, they can even make profit projections from it like on any other business venture. For them, that's all it is - another way to make a buck, lots of them.

The central thesis of this chapter is that giant transnational corporations today have become so dominant they now control our lives and the world, and they exploit both fully and ruthlessly. While they claim to be serving us and bringing us the fruits of the so-called "free market," in fact, they just use us for their gain. They've deceived us and highjacked the government to serve them as subservient proxies in their unending pursuit to dominate the world's markets, resources, cheap labor abroad and our own right here.

Predatory Behaviour

And they've done it much like what happens in the marketplace when a predator company attempts to take control of another one that prefers to remain independent. They launch a hostile takeover,

vittam eva kalau nrnam
janmacara-gunodayah
dharma-nyaya-vyavasthayam
karanam balam eva hi
In Kali-yuga, wealth alone will be considered the sign of a man's good birth, proper behavior and fine qualities. And law and justice will be applied only on the basis of one's power.
~ Srimad Bhagavatam (12.2.2)

going around or over the heads of the target's management, their employees and the communities they operate in. They go right to the target's shareholders and promise them a better deal, meaning a premium price on the stock they hold.

They do this, as in a friendly merger, for a variety of financial and strategic reasons, but essentially it's to achieve any possible immediate gain as well as over the longer term greater market dominance that will build future profits. But what happens in the wake of a takeover. Assets get stripped, spun-off and/or sold-off. Plants are closed. Jobs are lost. And all this is done for the primary bottom line goal - "the bottom line," higher profits, whatever the cost to people, communities or society.

A Destructive Force, Hostile To People, Societies And The Environment

Think of it this way. Large corporations today everywhere are a destructive force, hostile to people, societies and the environment. They're nothing less than legal private tyrannies operating freely with virtually no restraint. Everything for them, animal, vegetable or mineral, is viewed as a production input to be commodified and consumed for profit and then discarded when no longer of use.

And to achieve maximum profits, costs must be rigidly controlled. That means the lowest prices paid for goods and services, the lowest wages paid to workers (below privileged higher management who reward themselves richly), as little as possible spent on essential benefits like health care and pensions, and increasingly little or no concern about the long-term cost of exploiting, plundering or even destroying the natural environment and the future ability of the planet to sustain life. These issues, however recognized and grave, are for someone else to deal with later.

Though still considered "owners," stockholders in major public companies do not manage, fund, or accept liability for "their" corporations. Ownership function has shrunk to one dimension: extracting wealth.

The Bottom Line - Higher Profits

For now all that matters is today, the next quarter's earnings and keeping the stockholders and Wall Street happy. They only understand numbers on financial statements and are blind, unconcerned and even hostile to human and societal welfare or a safe environment that will protect and sustain all life forms. They call it "free market capitalism." It's really the law of the jungle. They're the predators, we're the prey, and every day they eat us alive.

Does all this make sense? And do corporate chieftains who live in a community, love their wives and children, contribute to charities, attend church and believe in its teachings really go to work every day and think - "who and what can I exploit today?" They sure do because they have no other choice. No more so than breathing in and breathing out.

How The Law Affects Corporate Behavior

Publicly owned corporations are mandated by law to serve only the interests of their shareholders and do it by working to maximize the value of their equity holdings by increasing profits. That's it. Case closed. Think of these businesses as gated communities of owners (large and small), the welfare of whom is all that matters

and the world outside the gates is to be used and exploited for that one purpose only.

Forget about any social responsibility or safeguarding the environment. The idea is to grow sales, keep costs low, increase profits, and if you do it well, shareholder value will rise, the owners and Wall Street will be happy, and you as a CEO or senior executive will probably get a raise, good bonus and keep your job.

Try being worker-friendly, a nice guy, a good citizen or a friend of the earth and fail to achieve the above objectives and you'll likely face dismissal and even possible shareholder lawsuit for not pursuing your fiduciary responsibility. Anyone choosing this line of work has no other choice. To do the job well, you have to think only of the care and feeding of your shareholders and the investment community,

But there's a reason, there's a reason. There's a reason for this. There's a reason education sucks and its the same reason it will never ever ever be fixed. Its never gonna get any better, don't look for it. Be happy with what you got, because the owners of this country don't want that. They don't want a population of citizens capable of critical thinking. They don't want well informed, well educated people capable of critical thinking. They're not interested in that.

~ George Carlin

ignore the law if that's what it takes to do it, and obey the only law that counts - the one that helps you grow the "bottom line."

There's No Government Of, For And By The People - It's A Democracy For The Privileged Elite

There's nothing in the Constitution, which is public law, that gives corporations the rights they've gotten. It never mattered to them. They just crafted their own private law, piece by piece, over many years with the help of corporate-friendly lawyers, legislators and the courts. And today it's easier than ever with both major parties strongly pro-business and the courts stacked with business-friendly judges ready to do their bidding.

The result is big business is now the paymaster, or puppetmaster, with government and the halls of justice their faithful servants. There's no government of, for and by the people, no public sovereignty, no democratic rights or any choices but to accept their authority and bow to their will. It's a democracy for the few alone - the privileged elite. Our only choice is to go along to get along or get out of their way.

Source

1,2, Thom Hartmann A, Jan. 2, 2014

Derber, C. 1998, Corporation nation: how corporations are taking over our lives and what we can do about it, St. Martin's Press, New York.

Donaldson, T. & Gini, A. 1996, Case studies in business ethics, 4th edn, Prentice Hall, Upper Saddle River, N.J.

Estes, R.W. 1996, Tyranny of the bottom line: why corporations make good people do bad things, 1st edn, Berrett-Koehler Publishers; San Francisco; Emeryville, CA.

Frederick, W.C. 2006, Corporation be good! : the story of corporate social responsibility, Dog Ear Pub., Indianapolis, IN.

Corporatocracy

Corporatocracy refers to a society dominated politically and economically by large corporations. A society turns into a corporatocracy when its economic and political systems are controlled by corporations or corporate interests.[1] It is a generally pejorative term often used by critics of the current economic situation in a particular country, especially the United States.[2][3]

This is different from corporatism, which is the organisation of society into groups with common interests. Economist Jeffrey Sachs described the United States as a corporatocracy in his book The Price of Civilization. [4] He suggested that it arose from four trends: weak national parties and strong political representation of individual districts, the large U.S. military establishment after World War II, big corporate money financing election campaigns, and globalization tilting the balance away from workers.[4]

CORPORATOCRACY
THE POWER OF CORPORATIONS OVER GOVERNMENT

This collective is what author C Wright Mills called the Power Elite, wealthy individuals who hold prominent positions in corporatocracies. They control the process of determining a society's economic and political policies. [18]

HYPOCRISY
HYPNOCRACY
CORPORATOCRACY

The concept has been used in explanations of bank bailouts, excessive pay for CEOs, as well as complaints such as the exploitation of national treasuries, people, and natural resources.[5] It has been used by critics of globalization,[6] sometimes in conjunction with criticism of the World Bank or unfair lending practices,[19] as well as criticism of "free trade agreements".[7]

Paying Their Way To Control

In US, corporate political donations have grown rapidly; in 2000, business interests donated $1.2 billion to federally elected candidates, accounting for 75% of all political donations. With 20,000 lobbyists in Washington, corporations have become experts

Separation of Corporation and State

at getting their money's worth in legislation and lax regulation in return for cash contributions.

In India, 90% of contributions to national parties come from corporates. In a sign of the rising role of the corporate sector in the nation's electoral process, reports submitted by national parties to the Election Commission (EC) show that 90 per cent of the donations received by them in 2013-14 were from corporates and business houses. Only 10 per cent donations were from individual sources.

According to an analysis by non-profit election watchdog Association of Democratic Reforms (ADR), of reports submitted to the EC, total donations received from four national parties — Congress, NCP, CPI(M) and CPI — rose by Rs.62.69 crore, an increase of 517 per cent from 2012-13.

"Ninety per cent of the donations being from corporates shows the increasing hold of the corporate sector on political parties, which is somewhat disconcerting," says Jagdeep Chhokar, founder trustee of ADR.

Reference

1."Corporatocracy". Oxford Dictionaries. .... a society or system that is governed or controlled by corporations.

2.Wikipedia, Jamie Reysen (October 4, 2011). "At Boston's Dewey Square, a protest of varied voices". Boston Globe. ... Corporatocracy is the new Fascism ...

What I may call the messages of Brave New World, but it is possible to make people contented with their servitude. I think this can be done. I think it has been done in the past. I think it could be done even more effectively now because you can provide them with bread and circuses and you can provide them with endless amounts of distractions and propaganda.

~ Aldous Huxley

3.Will Storey (October 6, 2011). "D.C. Occupied, More or Less". The New York Times..... we've surrendered our nation to a corporatocracy ...

4.Sachs, Jeffrey (2011). The Price of Civilization. New York: Random House. pp. 105, 106, 107.

5.John Perkins (March 2, 2011). "Ecuador: Another Victory for the People". Huffington Post.

6.Roman Haluszka (Nov 12, 2011). "Understanding Occupy's message". Toronto Star.

7.Andy Webster (August 14, 2008). "Thoughts on a 'Corporatocracy'". The New York Times.

Television is the most powerful weapon of psychological warfare in history. The programming that we are constantly assaulted by throughout our lives conditions us. It programs us to a particular worldview. Now, we may consider it normal because we were born into this system of lies and deception. And because we were born into this situation and our parents were born into it and have suffered from it, we don't know any better.

~ Steven Jacobson

6

A Profile

Of The World's Largest 200 Transnational Corporations

In December, 2000 The Institute for Policy Studies released a report called "The Rise of Corporate Global Power." It was a profile of the 200 largest transnationals that showed just how dominant they are. A summary of their findings is listed below.

1. Of the world's 100 largest economies, 51 are corporations.

2. The combined sales of these 200 corporations (called "The Group" below) in 1999 equalled 27.5% of world Gross Domestic Product (GDP) and are growing faster than overall global economic activity.

3. The Group's combined sales exceed the total combined economies of all nations in the world except the largest 10.

4. The Group's combined sales are 18 times the income of

We make you pay for the water you drink, for the food you eat, for the wars we need, for the crimes we commit; we make you dedicate the most important part of your life to us, but we give you wages and tell you they allow you to buy stuff and pay for your needs to make us even richer.
We call this freedom.

the bottom one fourth of the world's population (1.2 billion people) living in "severe" poverty.

5. Despite their combined size and percentage of world economic activity, The Group employs only 0.78% of the world's workforce.

6. From 1983 to 1999 The Group's workforce grew only 14.4% while their profits increased by 362.4% or about 25 times as much.

7. The largest employer in the world, Walmart, employed 1,140,000 in 1999 (1.6 million in 2005) or 5% of The Group's total employment. It's also a model (and increasingly a target) for corporate union-busting, widespread use of part-time workers and a practice of avoiding giving its workers needed benefits like health insurance.

8. 82 US corporations are in The Group, twice as many as Japan with 41, the next highest contributing country.

9. 44 of the US corporations in The Group didn't pay the full 35% federal tax rate from 1996 - 1998. 7 of them paid no tax in 1998 and also got tax rebates, including Enron and Worldcom now exposed as corporate criminals.

10. The percent of The Group's sales from the service sector (not manufacturing) grew from 33.8% in 1983 to 46.7% in 1999. In the US, the service sector comprised 79% of the total economy in 2004.

Reference
Stephen Lendman
Friedman, M. 1962, Capitalism and freedom, University of Chicago Press, Chicago.

Power of Tagline
If you look at Nike revenues, the big money set in consistently after 1989, the year of the great "Just do it." Did the words define the moment, or did they then drive the machine?

"There are some things money can't buy. For everything else, there's MasterCard." Without question, these twelve words reversed the fortunes of the brand. "Think small," "A diamond is forever," "Got milk?" Words you could take to the bank.

7

Corporations

The Real 'Weapons of Mass Destruction'

Although corporations aren't human, they can live forever, change their identity, reside in many places simultaneously in many countries, can't be imprisoned for wrongdoing and can change themselves into new persons at will for any reason. They have the same rights and protections as people under the Bill of Rights but not the responsibilities. From that right, corporations became unbound, free to grow and gain immense power and be able to become the dominant institution that now runs the country, the world and all our lives. Most important, they got an unwritten license from all three branches of the government to operate freely for their own benefit and others of their privileged class and do it at the public expense everywhere. They've exploited it fully as they're grown in size and dominance, and the result has been lives destroyed, the environment harmed and needless wars fought on their behalf because they open markets and grow profits. It's no

Is there any man, is there any woman, let me say any child here that does not know that the seed of war in the modern world is industrial and commercial rivalry?
~ Woodrow Wilson

exaggeration to say these institutions today are the real "weapons of mass destruction."

The planets's defense budget is in trillions and it mostly benefits the corporations. According to a report by The Center for Defense Information, since 1945, US alone has spent over $21 trillion on its military. And it's been done largely to benefit US corporations even though the country had no real enemies all through those years - except for the ones they attacked with no provocation or invented to scare the public so they'd buy into the scam that they needed industrial strength military spending for national security.

Ronald Reagan was very adept at scare tactics and duping the public. He fathered the Contra wars in the 80s in Nicaragua and scared half the public into believing the ruling Sandinista

government was a threat to invade Texas and threaten the whole country.

He tried and failed to get Mexican president Miguel de la Madrid to go along with him. The Mexican president said if he did 70 million Mexicans would die laughing. It's hard to believe the US public could ever fall for such a threat but they did. Although the nation was at peace during his tenure, Reagan expanded the military budget by 43% over what it was at the height of the Vietnam war (and ran up huge budget deficits doing it). The public suffered for it with the loss of social benefits, but business loved it and him, and the stock market took off on an 18 year bull run.

But after the 9/11 attack, the floodgates really opened wide. In fiscal year 2000 the military budget was $289 billion, but up it went steadily after that reaching $442 billion in 2006 and currently it is almost touching a trillion.

Add to that over $100 billion for Homeland Security (another public rip-off as part of a move toward a full-blown national security police state) and that kind of spending, with billions more available at the drop of an add-on presidential emergency request gives a whole new meaning to the term "war profiteer." And while the big defense contractors reap the biggest benefits, many thousands of US corporations are in on the take as the Pentagon is a big buyer of everything from expensive R & D and high tech weapons to breakfast cereals and toilet paper.

Using the false Bush slogan about leaving no child behind for his failed education program, the Pentagon for sure leaves no corporation behind in its generosity. Corporations wanting a piece of the action need only remember and abide by the scriptural message from John 16:24: "ask and you shall receive."

Most of humanity is in an absolute hypnotic trance that they're put in from cradle to grave by constant repetition of a fake reality and when we wake up from this then we will not be subservient.
~ David Icke

Here's the 2 key questions to ask. Does anyone feel safer, and who'll pick up the tab? The average worker doesn't share in those big tax cuts, his income is losing the war to inflation, his benefits are eroding, and someone some day has to pay that $18 trillion national debt that keeps rising $2.2 billion every day.

And along with that burden, the people have never been less safe, and they have to pay the bill because corporations never do. They're in another queue for more tax cuts, and public will see more social benefits cut to pay for them too. In the political game of musical chairs, corporations get them all every time, and the public is always left standing (out in the cold).

Reference

Stephen Lendman

Robert Koehler (December 18, 2011). The language of empire:, Baltimore Sun.

Population Action International: "The Security Demographic: Population and Civil Conflict after the Cold War"

What is the advancement over the dogs? This destruction of another nation by nuclear bombs is the dogs' mentality. Sometimes, even when chained by their respective masters, two dogs will fight as soon as they meet. Have you seen it? It's no better than that.

—*Srila Prabhupada (Lecture, Melbourne, Australia)*

8

Inventing Wars

Once the cold war ended after the Berlin wall came down and the Soviet Union became 15 independent republics, there was some hope for a peace dividend - meaning less for the military and more social spending. That wasn't what the first Bush administration and Pentagon had in mind as they frantically searched for and easily found new potential enemies as a way to make the case for continued militarized state capitalism.

Their language manipulation experts came up with and sold to the Congress and public the threat of "growing technological sophistication of Third World conflicts" which "will place serious demands on our forces" and "continue to threaten US interests," even without "the backdrop of superpower competition." Our defense strategy would thus be based on maintaining global "stability" (more code language meaning assuring obedience to US dominance).

In the 1990 National Security Strategy, the Pentagon presented its defense budget to the Congress using the above stated pretext to justify what they wanted. It called for strengthening "the defense industrial base" (code language for the high-tech industry in all its forms) through generous subsidies as incentives "to invest in new facilities and equipment as well as in research and development."

They got what they wanted, and it set off the high tech stock market boom that lasted until the speculative bubble burst in March,

2000 when the economy slowed and slipped into recession. Three years later in a post 9/11 environment, the economy was again growing as was annual defense spending, and the stock market began another ascent that's so far continuing.

The many corporations now benefitting from Pentagon largesse are so addicted to it that they become the main promoters of and cheerleaders for conflicts or preparations for them because they guarantee bigger handouts that are so good for business.

It's a dirty business, but isn't that the fundamental predatory nature of large-scale capitalism that relies on a state policy of imperialism to thrive and prosper. Senator Henry Cabot Lodge explained it in 1895, in an unguarded moment, when he said "commerce follows the flag." He might have added that the flag also follows commerce.

The great political economist Harry Magdoff, who died this year on New Year's day, also explained it well in his 1969 book The Age of Imperialism when he wrote: "Imperialism is not a matter of choice for a capitalist society; it is the way of life of such a society."

And historian Henry Steele Commager wrote about how a national security police state and its bureaucracy lends its great talents and resources "not to devising ways of reducing tensions and

People don't want wars

Politicians, bankers and corporations do

avoiding war, but to ways of exacerbating tensions and preparing for war."

The reason, of course, is because war is so good for business. Since 9/11, along with all their other largesse and waste, the Pentagon outsourced on average $250 billion a year in work to corporations. Almost half of it was in no-bid contracts and three fourths of that was to the five largest defense contractors headed by Lockheed Martin and Boing. L-M is the undisputed king of contractors. They literally run the enterprise of empire from the inside and out. They're not only its biggest beneficiary, they also help shape the policy guaranteeing it - to the tune of $65 million every day. And they collect their loot even when their killing machines don't work right.

MEN IN SUITS KILL MORE PEOPLE THAN MEN IN UNIFORM

Then, of course, there's Halliburton and Bechtel. They're always big time winners in the handout sweepstakes. These two well-connected companies have been at the head of the queue in the

stri-bala-go-dvija-ghnas ca para-dara-dhanadrtah
uditasta-mita-praya alpa-sattvalpakayusah
asamskrtah kriya-hina rajasa tamasavrtah
prajas te bhaksayisyanti mleccha rajanya-rupinah
These barbarians in the guise of kings will devour the citizenry, murdering innocent women, children, cows and brahmanas and coveting the wives and property of other men. They will be erratic in their moods, have little strength of character and be very short-lived. Indeed, not purified by any Vedic rituals and lacking in the practice of regulative principles, they will be completely covered by the modes of passion and ignorance.
~ Srimad Bhagavatam (12.1.39-40)

looting of Iraq and the US Treasury. They've gotten huge no-bid contracts worth many billions which they then freely supplemented with gross (read: criminal) overcharges and gotten away with most of it. And we can't ignore the notorious Carlyle Group, the nation's largest privately held defense contractor with the tightest of ties right to the Oval Office.

Reference

Stephen Lendman

Marc Pilisuk; Jennifer Achord Rountree (2008). Who Benefits from Global Violence and War: Uncovering a Destructive System. Greenwood Publishing Group.

"Stop the War Coalition: Timeline of Events 2001–2011"

Heinsohn, G.(2005): "Population, Conquest and Terror in the 21st Century."

"Darkness of the present age is not due to a lack of material advancement, but that we have lost the clue to our spiritual advancement, which is the prime necessity of human life, the criterion of the highest type of human civilization. Throwing of bombs from airplanes is no advancement of civilization from the primitive, uncivilized practice of dropping big stones on enemies' heads from the tops of hills. . . "

— *Srila Prabhupada (Lecture, February 1936, Bombay)*

9

The Downward Trajectory

Of Ordinary Workers

Over the past generation working people have seen an unprecedented fall in their standard of living. In the past (except for periods of economic downturn), workers saw their wages and benefits grow each year and their living standards improve. Today it's just the opposite. Adjusted for inflation, the average working person earns less than 30 years ago, and even with modest annual increases is not keeping up with inflation.

Some of the world data is especially shocking. According to the UN 2002 Human Development Report, the richest 1% in 1999-2000 received as much income as the bottom 57% combined, over 45% of the world's population lived then on less than $2 a day, about 40% had no sanitation services and about 840 million people were malnourished. In addition, 1 in 6 grade school children were not in school, and half the global nonagricultural labor force was either unemployed or underemployed.

Most shocking and disturbing of all is that many millions (likely tens of millions) of people in the less developed world die each year from starvation and treatable diseases because of abuse and/or neglect by rich nations that could prevent it. And these numbers reflect the state of things at the end of a decade of overall impressive economic growth. But it shows how those gains went mainly to a privileged upper class who got them at the expense of the majority below them especially the most desperate and needy.

The Richest Country In The World - An Appraisal

In December, 2004 the New York Times reported the US ranked 49th in world literacy, and the US Department of Labor estimates over 20% of the population is functionally illiterate (compared to about 1% in Venezuela and Cuba, two of the countries they demonize the most). It's also true that the quality of public education has been in decline in urban schools for many years.

In addition the extent of racial segregation is now as great as in the 1960s, despite supposed but unrealized gains from the civil rights legislation of that time. Further, state and local education budgets aren't keeping up with a growing need or are being cut. A growing number of lwer income students are now deprived of a chance for higher education - and it's getting steadily worse.

The World Health Organization ranked the US 37th in the world in "overall health performance" and 54th in the fairness of health care. And in 2004 about 46 million people had no health insurance

and millions more were underinsured. These appalling numbers are in spite of the fact that the US spends far more on health care per capita than any other country. And all developed countries in the world, except the US and South Africa, provide free health care for all its citizens paid for through taxes.

WORK vs. PRISON

Just in case you ever got the two mixed up, this should make things a bit more clear..

IN PRISON ... you spend the majority of your time in an 8X10 cell;

AT WORK ... you spend the majority of your time in a 6X8 cubicle

IN PRISON ... you get three meals a day;

AT WORK ... you only get a break for one meal and you have to pay for it.

IN PRISON ... you get time off for good behavior;

AT WORK...you get rewarded for good behavior with more work.

IN PRISON ... the guard locks and unlocks all the doors for you;

AT WORK ... you must carry around a security card and open all the doors for yourself.

IN PRISON ... you can watch TV and play games;

AT WORK ... you get fired for watching TV and playing games.

IN PRISON ... you get your own toilet;

AT WORK ... you have to share with some idiot who pees on the seat.

IN PRISON ... they allow your family and friends to visit;

AT WORK ... you can't even speak to your family.

IN PRISON ... all expenses are paid by the taxpayers with no work required.

AT WORK ... you get to pay all the expenses to go to work and then they deduct taxes from your salary to pay for prisoners.

IN PRISON ... you spend most of your life looking through bars from inside wanting to get out.

AT WORK ... you spend most of your time wanting to get out and go inside bars.

IN PRISON ... you must deal with sadistic wardens;

AT WORK... they are called managers.

The European Dream reported US childhood poverty ranked 22nd or second to last among developed nations.

The New York Times reported 12 million American families, over 10% of all households, struggle to feed themselves.

The NYT also reported the US ranks 41st in world infant mortality.

All this and many more depressing statistics are happening in the richest country in the world with a 2005 Gross Domestic Product of $12.5 trillion.

The dramatic effects of social inequality in the US are seen in the Economic Policy Institute's 2004 report on the State of Working America." It shows the top 1% controls more than one-third of the nation's wealth while the bottom 80% have 16%. Even worse, the top 20% holds 84% of all wealth while the poorest 20% are in debt and owe more than they own.

Corporate Gain Has Come at the Cost of Worker Loss

Not coincidentally, as workers have seen their living standards decline, transnational corporations have experienced unprecedented growth and dominance. And that trend continues unabated.

Ahara-nidra-bhaya-maithuna, eating, sleeping, mating and defending. These are physical necessities. So these physical necessities, if you study, amongst the animals, they have no problem. But as yesterday we were talking, in the human society, they have created problem. Nobody knows where to eat. These hotels means, increase in number of hotels means that people have no fixed place to live. Today in this hotel, the next day, another hotel. Then so many restaurants means people have no fixed place where to eat. In India still, because they are not so materially advanced, even the poorest man has got some certain fixed up place, his cottage, he has got his wife, he has got his child, and he works, whatever he can do. He lives peacefully still, in the village, although he hasn't got very gorgeous dress and motorcar. But he's peaceful. You'll find still.

~ Srila Prabhupada (Srimad-Bhagavatam 1.16.23 -- Hawaii, January 19, 1974

How and why is this happening? Begin with the most business-friendly governments the country has had over the last 25 years since the "roaring" 1920s when President Calvin Coolidge explained that "the business of America is business."

He, and two other Republican presidents then did everything they could to help their business friends. But they were small-timers compared to today, and the size, dominance and global reach of big business then was a small fraction of what it is now. And back then, job "outsourcing", GATT and WTO type trade agreements, and the concept of globalization weren't in the vocabulary.

Now they're central to the problem as they've created a severe class divide (not to mention the developing world where it's far worse) that keep widening.

Reference
Stephen Lendman
We Are The 99.9%, Paul Krugman, New York Times, November 24, 2011.
Carl Gibson (November 2, 2011). "The Corporatocracy Is the 1 Percent"
The Distribution of US Wealth, Capital Income and Returns since 1913, Emmanuel Saez, Gabriel Zucman

10

Obscene Profits

Worker loss has been corporations' gain - big time. In 2004 the world's largest 500 corporations posted their highest ever revenues and profits - an astonishing $14.9 trillion in revenue and $731.2 billion in profits. And top corporate officials are raking it in, rewarding themselves with obscene amounts of salaries, bonuses in the multi-millions and lucrative stock options worth even more for many of them.

That level of largesse is only possible at the expense of working people here and everywhere. Oliver Stone may have been thinking of them when he made his 1980s film, Wall Street. In it was the memorable line spoken by the character portraying the manipulative investor/deal-maker when he explained that "greed is good."

Except for two brief and mild recessions, corporations have prospered since the 1980s in a very business-friendly environment. The result has been rising profits to record levels, enhanced even more by generous corporate tax cuts (and personal ones as well mostly for the rich).

In US, especially after the election of George Bush, corporations have never had it better. It's been so good that 82 of the largest 275 companies paid no federal income tax in at least one year from 2001-2003 or got a refund; 28 of them got tax rebates in all 3 of those years even though their combined profits totaled $44.9 billion; 46 of them, earning $42.6 billion in profits, paid no tax in 2003 and got $4.9 billion back in tax rebates. And the average CEO pay for these 46 companies in 2004 was $12.6 million.

Along with big tax cuts and generous rebates, big corporations are on the government dole big time in the form of subsidies, otherwise known as "corporate welfare." It's also known as socialism for the rich (and capitalism for the rest of us).

In 1997 the Fortune 500 companies got $75 billion in "public aid" even though they earned record profits of $325 billion. They got it in many forms - grants, contracts, loans and loan guarantees and lots more. Today there are about 125 business subsidy programs in the US federal budget benefitting all major areas of business.

Some examples of this government largesse include:

Selling the rights to billions of dollars of oil, gas, coal and other mineral reserves at a small fraction of their market value.

The giveaway of the entire broadcast spectrum to the corporate media.

The country is governed for the richest, for the corporations, the bankers, the land speculators, and for the exploiters of labor. The majority of mankind are working people. So long as their fair demands – the ownership and control of their livelihoods – are set at naught, we can have neither men's rights nor women's rights. The majority of mankind is ground down by industrial oppression in order that the small remnant may live in ease.
~ Helen Keller

Charging mostly corporate ranchers (including big oil and insurance companies) dirt cheap grazing rates on millions of acres of public land.

Spending many billions of dollars on R & D and handing over the results to corporations free of charge. "Big Pharma" is notorious for letting government do their expensive research and then cashing in on the results by soaking the public with sky-high prices and rigging the game with through WTO rules that get them exclusive patent rights for 20 years or longer when they're able to extend them through the courts.

Giving the nuclear industry billions in handouts and guaranteeing government protection to pick up the cost in case of any serious accidents that otherwise might cost the company affected billions and possibly bankrupt it.

Giving corporate agribusiness producers many billions in annual subsidies.

Ordinary public, the individual taxpayers, pay the bill for this generosity. But we actually pay these corporations twice - first through our taxes and then for the cost of their products and services. And they don't even thank us.

Reference

Stephen Lendman

Are You Rich Enough? The Terrible Tragedy of Income Inequality Among The 1%, Forbes, November 25, 2013

yada mayanrtam tandra
nidra himsa visadanam
soka-mohau bhayam dainyam
sa kalis tamasah smrtah
When there is a predominance of cheating, lying, sloth, sleepiness, violence, depression, lamentation, bewilderment, fear and poverty, that age is Kali, the age of the mode of ignorance.
~ *Srimad Bhagavatam (12.3.30)*

How You, I, and Everyone Got The Top 1 Percent All Wrong, Derek Thompson, The Atlantic, March 30, 2014

Financial Times-U.S. Share Buybacks and Dividends Hit Record-June 18, 2014

11

You Are Not An American or Indian Citizen

You Are A Corporate Citizen

Modern Imperialism - The Corporate Takeover of the World

According to Noreena Hertz, over the last three decades the balance of power between politics and commerce has shifted radically, leaving politicians increasingly subordinate to the colossal economic power of big business. Unleashed by the Thatcher-Reagan axis, and accelerated by the end of the Cold War, this process has grown Hydra-like over the last two decades and now manifests itself in diverse forms. Whichever way we look at it, corporations are taking on the responsibilities of government.

And as business has extended its role, it has actually come to define the public realm. The political state has become the corporate state. Governments are shattering the implicit contract between state and citizen that lies at the heart of a democratic society.

All over the world, concerns are being raised about governments' loyalties and corporations' objectives. Concerns that the pendulum of capitalism may have swung just a bit too far; that our love affair with the free market may have obscured harsh truths; that too many are losing out. That the state cannot be trusted to look after our interests; and that we are paying too high a price for our increased economic growth. They are worried that the sound of business is drowning out the voices of the people. ~ Noreena Hertz (Global Capitalism and the Death of Democracy)

Pursuing a policy of neo-colonialism, the multinational corporations infringe up on the sovereignty of the Third World countries, seek to gain control over their natural resources, impose unequal agreements upon them and impede the development of their independent national economies.

Imperialists, like everyone else, have always sought to justify their actions. In the latter 19th Century and the early decades of the 20th Century, imperialism was more direct than it is today, and it was called imperialism. The basic concept was rather simple. A militarily strong country from Europe would enter a militarily weak third world country and take control of it. The natural resources and human labor of the weaker country were put in the service of the stronger country.

'White Man's Burden'

The justification of this process has been captured by the phrase "white man's burden". Under this theme, imperialism was justified on the basis that the dominated countries were inhabited by culturally backwards savages who were in need of being "civilized".

Dominating them was not something that the imperialists did in order to enrich themselves, but rather it was a burden that they carried out for strictly 'altruistic purposes'.

Numerous successful rebellions by the colonized countries in the first half of the 20th Century eventually discredited the concept, so that imperialism went out of favor. The new anti-imperialist

"I have traveled across the length and breath of India and I have not seen one person who is a beggar, who is a thief, such wealth I have seen in this country, such high moral values, people of such caliber (of noble character), that I do not think we would ever conquer this country...........unless we break the very backbone of this nation which is her spiritual and cultural heritage."

-Lord MCLau, British colonial, on February 2, 1835

world attitude towards imperialism is captured in the preamble to the United Nations Charter, which came into existence in 1945:

We the people of the United Nations determined:

To save succeeding generations from the scourge of war, which twice in our lifetime has brought untold sorrow to mankind, and

To reaffirm faith in fundamental human rights, in the dignity and worth of the human person, in the equal rights of men and women and of nations large and small, and

To establish conditions under which justice and respect for the obligations arising from treaties and other sources of international law can be maintained, and

To promote social progress and better standards of life in larger freedom.

But progress has never followed a straight line. Imperialism is alive and well in the world today, but it goes under different names, such as "free trade", "foreign investment", or "structural adjustment".

Naomi Klein, in her book, "The Shock Doctrine – The Rise of Disaster Capitalism", uses another name for it: Shock therapy. As always has been the case, its practitioners and proponents provide justifications for the new imperialism, just as they did for the old imperialism. But of course they use different justifications than the old ones, in order to conform to the new ideologies.

One of the ideologies at the root of all these policies is supplied by Milton Friedman's economic theories, developed at the University of Chicago. These theories, when put into practice in several countries over more than three decades, have served primarily to increase the wealth and power of the wealthy, at the expense of everyone else.

Invading The World - One Economy At A Time

Antonia Juhasz, in her book, "The Bush Agenda – Invading the World One Economy at a Time", describes how force and violence are used by third world governments to protect corporate interests:

"Cochabamba is the 3rd largest city in Bolivia. In late 1999, the World Bank required that Bolivia privatize Cochabamba's water in return for reduction of its debts. Bechtel – one of the top ten water privatization companies in the world – won the contract.

Immediately after Bechtel took over the Cochabamba water system, and before any of the promised investments in infrastructure were made to improve or expand services, the company raised the price of water by 100%... Many were simply forced to do without running water. The same law that privatized the water system also privatized any collected water, including rainwater collected in barrels.

The majority of the people voted for the cancellation of the contract with Bechtel. When this demand was met with silence from government officials, the citizens went on a citywide strike. The Bolivian government defended Bechtel's right to privatize by sending armed military troops into the streets to disperse the crowds. At least one 17-year-old boy was shot and killed and hundreds more were injured."

Petras describes the role of the U.S. military as the ultimate guarantee that their preferred policies will be realized:

'The responsibility of the US for the growth of Latin American billionaires and mass poverty is several-fold and involves a very wide gamut of political institutions, business elites and academic and media moguls. First and foremost the US backed the military dictators and Neoliberal politicians who set up the billionaire economic models.'

The New Imperialism

Under the new imperialism, various strict and related conditions are imposed upon a country in return for a loan, usually structured by international financial institutions that are largely under the control of the United States. In addition to a strict schedule for repaying of the loan, the conditions generally include: opening the country to private investment; the privatization of national resources, services, and industries; various favors towards those industries, like selling off state assets at bargain prices, tax breaks, subsidies, a paucity of regulation, and laws that greatly favor capital over labor; and drastic cuts in social services for the country's inhabitants.

The primary result is that the foreign corporations and investors make vast profits while the country's inhabitants become even more impoverished than they were. The process is something akin to loan sharking.

The rationalization used to justify this process is that the privatized industries, through the process of the unfettered "free market", will be far more efficient and productive than they were when they were under government ownership. This will result in improved goods and services for the country's inhabitants, and will provide tons of jobs as well. However, it rarely works like that.

The bottom line is that rather than serving as a financial asset to the country, profits accrue to the MNC and its investors while draining the country of its financial and other resources.

Foreign investors have successfully secured control over some of the most lucrative oil and gas fields from compliant rulers. The obvious result has been a huge transfer of wealth from the national economy to the MNCs under the assumption that the new investments will provide compensatory benefits. The problem is that energy corporations are notorious for not fulfilling their investment obligations.

Why Do Countries Allow This To Happen To Them?

Payoffs

These corporations have given rise to a big question mark whether political freedom will continue to exist when economic power is getting more and more concentrated in fewer and fewer hands.

They lobby for a particular interest. They finance individual members of a political party and parties themselves in elections.

"The liberty of a democracy is not safe if the people tolerate the growth of private power to a point where it becomes stronger than the democratic state itself. That in its essence is fascism: ownership of government by an individual, by a group or any controlling private power." ~President Franklin D. Roosevelt.

These days money plays a major role in elections. Any party that can manipulate funds has better chances of victory. Naturally they get political control of the developing countries.

In this context we can mention Lockheed scandal in which top officials in Western European countries and Japan were involved. When the facts came to light, the Japanese Prime Minister had to resign on corruption charges in the aeroplanes deal.

Dr. V. Gauri Shanker makes startling disclosures in his research thesis, "Taming the Giants: Transnational Corporation" which he wrote under the auspices of Jawaharlal Nehru University.

He writes how the Multinationals operating in India and Indonesia set apart secret funds for bribing officials and making political contributions. Sometimes the Multinationals act as fronts for their governments and interfere in the internal affairs of the host countries and cause political destabilization.

Persuasion

Persuasion is often the preferred initial method to convince countries to accept the conditions required by international lending institutions. Persuasion of course is apt to be more effective when countries are desperate for money. And it can take many forms.

The Multinationals concerned with food have succeeded in weaning the developing countries away from grain production so that they could make profitable grain exports to them.

On the land so released from food, the Multinationals themselves set up frontal vegetable growing business, earning big profits by exporting these items back to the West.

Mexico, which once grow a variety of local food grains, has been converted into an exporter of fruits and vegetables.

First there are the ideological arguments about the wonders of the "free market". Such arguments may have held some sway with well meaning people in the past. However, by now the fallacy of these arguments has become well known, as least among those who have studied their effects on developing countries.

John Perkins, in "Confessions of an Economic Hit Man", explains how persuasion is often used, from the perspective of an insider who formerly did the dirty work that he describes in his book. Perkins explains that economic hit men (EHM) are paid by multinational corporations to develop economic projections for major development projects in third world countries. Their projections are supposed to predict substantial economic growth and thereby justify huge loans from international lending institutions. The money from the loan then is immediately funneled into U.S. oil, engineering or construction companies (which is a precondition of the loan) to develop their projects.

Sometimes there are darker aspects to persuasion, for which we will probably never know the full extent. Perkins describes these aspects in his second book, "The Secret History of the American Empire – Economic Hit Men, Jackals, and the Truth about Global Corruption", quoting an anonymous source, who was a fellow EHM:

"I walked into El Presidente's office two days after he was elected and congratulated him. I said "Mr. President, in here I got a couple of hundred million dollars for you and your family, if you play the game – you know, be kind to my friends who run the oil companies, treat your Uncle Sam good." Then I stepped closer, reached my right hand into the other pocket, bent down next to his face, and whispered, "In here I got a gun and a bullet with your name on it – in case you decide to keep your campaign promises." I stepped back, sat down, and recited a little list for him, of presidents who were assassinated or overthrown because they defied their Uncle Sam: from Diem to Torrijos – you know the routine. He got the message."

'The business of America is business.'
~1920s US President Calvin Coolidge's dictum

Financial Manipulation Or Indifference

Naomi Klein explains in her book that countries are much more susceptible to requests to alter their laws and economic policies to benefit foreign corporations when they are in shock. The shock can result from war, assassination or overthrow of a head-of-state, natural disaster, or financial calamity. In any of these cases, the shock can provide great opportunities for opportunistic foreign scavengers.

The Southeast Asian financial crisis of 1997 – the economic collapse of the so-called Asian Tigers – provides a good example of how international financial institutions have used their financial powers to facilitate a financial crisis to benefit powerful corporations. Just prior to their collapse, the Asian Tigers were being held up as great success stories of globalization. Klein explains the role of international financial institutions in the crisis.

In the mid-nineties, under pressure from the IMF and the newly created World Trade Organization, Asian governments agreed to lift barriers to their financial sectors, allowing a surge of paper investing and currency trading.

As for the IMF, the world body created to prevent crashes like this one, it took the 'do-nothing approach' that had become its trademark since Russia. It did eventually respond – but not with the sort of fast, emergency stabilization loan that a purely financial crisis demanded. Instead, it came up with a long list of demands,

Multinationals have been exploiting the Third World countries in the field of pharmaceuticals.

This is particularly the in case of India. Such Multinationals have been propagating the use of non-essential drugs and making large profits through over-pricing. An expert committee insists that of the 43,600 drugs registered and sold in India, three-fourths are non-essential.

A survey conducted by the Indian Council of Medical Research points out that seven out of every ten purchases of antibiotics made in India are uncalled for.

Recently, there was a controversy over the multinationals marking and selling non-essential baby foods in India.

pumped up by the Chicago School certainty that Asia's catastrophe was an opportunity in disguise.

Klein also explains in great detail the motivation for the financial elites wanting the Asian economies to fail. Here is part of that explanation:

> If the crisis was left to worsen, all foreign currency would be drained from the region and Asian-owned companies would have either to close down or to sell themselves to Western firms.

The IMF was exclusively focused on how the crisis could be used as leverage. The meltdown had forced a group of strong-willed countries to beg for mercy; to fail to take advantage of that window of opportunity was, for the Chicago School economists running the IMF, tantamount to professional negligence.

To 'take advantage of the opportunity' the IMF required the Asian countries to adopt a host of Milton Friedman's Chicago School economic 'reforms':

> The IMF also demanded that the governments make deep budget cuts, leading to mass layoffs of public sector workers in countries where

In line with historic conflicts all over the world, the current battle is between the global public and the corporate and political elite over the control of government. Who decides how people organize and live their lives? Who decides if people go with or without water, food, healthcare or education? These rights must rest with the global public and their representative bodies, and not with a tiny minority who directly benefit from an ideology that shrinks public involvement in these central decisions.

Corporations are not people. They do not exist without shareholders and they exist only for profit. They are incapable of demonstrating the same values that people hold and express within their communities. The national constitution was never meant to represent the rights of economic entities; there is no mention of corporations or other such entities in the constitution of any country. The corporation must not enjoy the protection of the Bill of Rights. In a true democracy, corporations must exist at the pleasure of the people and under their sovereignty, not the other way round .

people were already taking their own lives in record numbers. They were now ready to be reborn, Chicago-style: privatized basic services, independent central banks, low social spending and, of course, total free trade. Indonesia would cut food subsidies.

Government Overthrow

John Perkins explains that if the EHMs are unsuccessful in their efforts to convince a government to play ball, then the "jackals" are sent in to assassinate or overthrow the uncooperative government officials in question, as was done for example in Iran in 1953, Guatemala in 1954, inChile in 1973, or in Indonesia in 1965.

Naomi Klein describes how Milton Freidman's economic theories and policies worked in tandem with U.S. covert assistance to destroy the economic functioning of several South American countries in the 1970s, following the overthrow of Salvador Allende and his replacement by the brutal dictator Augusto Pinochet in 1973:

'The Chicago School counterrevolution quickly spread. Brazil was already under the control of a U.S. supported junta. Friedman traveled to Brazil in 1973, at the height of that regime's brutality, and declared the economic experiment a "miracle". In Uruguay the military had staged a coup in 1973 and the following year decided to go the Chicago route. The effect on Uruguay's previously egalitarian society was immediate: real wages decreased by 28% and hordes of scavengers appeared on the streets. Next to join the experiment was Argentina in 1976, when a junta seized power from Isabel Peron. That meant that Argentina, Chile, Uruguay and Brazil – the countries that had been showcases of developmentalism – were now all run by U.S. backed military governments and were living laboratories of Chicago School economics.'

Violence And War

Violence and war blend with government overthrow as a means of getting countries to go along with their wishes. Perkins explains that when other methods don't work, then they send in the military, as they did in Panama in 1989 or in Iraq in 1991 and 2003.

Klein explains that the preferred economic policies are often so painful to a country's population, that peaceful means are not enough to maintain them. She describes the role of systematic violence in persuading Chileans to accept new economic policies following the installation of Pinoche's regime:

'The generals knew that their hold on power depended on Chileans being truly terrified. The trail of blood left behind over those four days came to be known as the Caravan of Death. In short order the entire country had gotten the message: resistance is deadly. In all, more than 3,200 people disappeared or were executed, at least 80,000 were imprisoned, and 200,000 fled the country.'

Examples Of The Consequences Of New Imperialism

The books described above provide numerous examples of the consequences of new imperialism in a wide range of countries. Here are just a few of them:

Russia 1991

Following the break-up of the Soviet Union, Russia was in dire financial straights as it attempted to convert to capitalism. Under pressure from the United States and international financial institutions, Boris Yeltsin decided to go the economic shock therapy route:

After only one year, shock therapy had taken a devastating toll: millions of middle-class Russians had lost their life savings when money lost its value, and abrupt cuts to subsidies meant millions of workers had not been paid in months. The average Russian consumed 40% less in 1992 than in 1991, and a third of the population fell below the poverty line. The middle class was forced to sell personal belongings from card tables on the streets.

Chile 1973

As described in Klein's book, following the overthrow of Allende and his replacement by Pinochet:

In 1974, inflation reached 375%. The cost of basics such as bread went through the roof. At the same time, Chileans were being thrown out of work because Pinochet's experiment with "free trade" was flooding the country with cheap imports. Unemployment hit record levels and hunger became rampant. Chicago boys argued that the problem didn't lie with their theory but with the fact that it wasn't being applied with sufficient strictness.

Poland - 1988

Poland won its independence from the Soviet Union in 1988, and it was in dire financial straights at that time. It was made clear to them that they could expect little or no help unless they agreed to economic shock therapy. Klein describes how that worked out:

Shock therapy in Poland did not cause "momentary dislocations," as predicted. It caused a full-blown depression: a 30% reduction in industrial production, unemployment skyrocketed, and in 1993 it reached 25% in some areas – a wrenching change in a country that, under Communism, for all its many abuses and hardships, had no open joblessness.

In 1989, 15% of Poland's population was living below the poverty line; in 2003, 59% of Poles had fallen below the line. Shock therapy, which eroded job protection and made daily life far more expensive, was not the route to Poland's becoming one of Europe's "normal" countries.

Three hundred multinational corporations now account for 25 per cent of the world's assets. The annual values of sales of each of the six largest transnational corporations, varying between $111 and $126 billion, are now exceeded by the GDPs of only twenty-one nation states.

Corporate sales account for two thirds of world trade and a third of world output (Coca-Cola, Toyota and Ford derive nearly half of their revenues outside their base in the USA), while as much as 40 per cent of world trade now occurs within multinational corporations. ~ Noreena Hertz

The Asian Tigers – 1997

Klein describes what happened to the Asian people following the financial crisis described above:

> 24 million people lost their jobs in this period. What disappeared in these parts of Asia was what was so remarkable about the region's "miracle" in the first place: its large and growing middle class. 20 million Asians were thrown into poverty in this period of what Rodolfo Walsh would have called "planned misery". Women and children suffered the worst of the crisis. Many rural families in the Philippines and South Korea sold their daughters to human traffickers who took them to work in the sex trade. The crisis saw a 20 percent increase in child prostitution.

Iraq – 2003

Antonia Juhasz explains in her book that economic plunder was one of the chief reasons, and probably the chief reason, for the U.S. invasion and occupation of Iraq. In that sense, it was a great success, not the failure that it is often made out to be.

The Foreign Investment Order provided the legal framework for the invasion of U.S. corporations into Iraq. It provided for the privatization of Iraq's state-owned enterprises, foreign ownership of Iraqi businesses, tax-free remittance of all profits, immunity of foreign businesses from Iraqi courts, and much else. As with everything else about the U.S. occupation, these provisions did great damage to the Iraqi people, for the benefit of U.S. corporations. Juhasz describes the effects of privatization of Iraqi industries:

> In Bremer's own words, "Restructuring inefficient state enterprises requires laying off workers.". Even those workers who still had jobs in Iraq at the time only received about half of what they made before the war. At the same time, prices skyrocketed.

Human civilizations should depend on the production of material nature without artificially attempting economic development to turn the world into a chaos of artificial greed and power only for the purpose of artificial luxuries and sense gratification. This is but the life of dogs and hogs.
~ Srila Prabhupada (Srimad Bhagavatam 1.10.4)

And with respect to the lack of any constraints on foreign corporations:

U.S. corporations are therefore invited to enter the Iraqi economy, exploit a nation at its most vulnerable point, with no obligation to reinvest in the country at a time when rebuilding Iraq is professed to be the Bush administration's most vital assignment. U.S. corporations have reaped staggering revenues from their Iraqi operations. Chevron, Bechtel, and Halliburton have each experienced skyrocketing returns to their Iraqi endeavors.

In the hands of U.S. corporations, the effort to rebuild Iraq was a miserable failure:

The Bush administration failed in this mission because it did not focus its efforts on the immediate provision of needs, but rather on the opening of Iraq to private foreign corporations. Iraqis have continually pointed to the lack of electricity as a primary source of unrest. Electricity has remained far below prewar levels and significantly below U.S. stated goals.

The result was frequent blackouts and the availability of electricity for only a few hours a day, with air conditioning unavailable much of the time in the face of outside temperatures of 130 degrees. Lack of potable water and sewage treatment has been another continuing and major problem:

The full failure of the reconstruction was revealed in a January 2006 U.S. government audit. Although more than 93% of the U.S. appropriation has been spent or committed to specific companies and projects, as much as 60% of all water and sewer projects will not be completed.

Why So Much Concern About Multinationals?

Big business elicits strong reactions. In his book The Corporation, now a successful television series and film, the Canadian academic Joel Bakan argues that the corporation is 'a pathological institution, a dangerous possessor of the great power it wields over people and societies'. The multinational corporation, because of its apparent mobility and assumed lack of loyalty to any one jurisdiction, is particularly mistrusted. But how did this mistrust come about?

In Europe, the controversy surrounding multinationals can be traced back to the post-war years. This was a time of huge expansion for corporations, particularly those originating in the USA. Many Europeans were beginning to resent the level of reliance by local industry on US foreign investment and worried, too, about the 'Americanisation' of culture, tastes and management methods. By the late 1960s, opposition to US-owned multinationals was high, as evidenced by the popularity of books critical of the 'American invasion'.

In the USA, on the other hand, multinationals appear to have been regarded relatively benignly by the public until the 1960s. But by this time the reputation of corporate America had begun to wane, as Hood vividly describes:

The privilege of influencing policy is one that rightly belongs to the public, not the corporate elite who make up less than 1% of the population. But since political influence increases with economic and financial power, the corporate influence in national and global governance structures far outweighs public influence. Thus, democratic process has been the battle ground whereupon the pubic good has fought the corporate agenda. Only when the global public seize back the democratic process and implement appropriate measures to curb corporate influence on the democratic process will the global economy reflect the needs of the majority.

The public's attention in many western countries has turned away from government – a fact born out by the very low turnouts during recent elections in the UK and US. Such national apathy to government is to a large extent the result of the failure of political leadership to sincerely represent the public or to convince the public that they are on their side, fighting for public issues. The resulting consensus within society adds momentum to the private sector's ambitions to roll back government control in favour of market forces. It has also contributed to the strengthening of the 'partnership' between the government and the business sector, and this has made it even easier for corporations to successfully lobby governmental to loosen their hold on the economy.

Investigative journalism became a heroic, even romantic, calling, with the name of the game being to catch greedy corporations in the act of polluting the water, selling shoddy and overpriced products, exploiting workers and families, and sacrificing the public's health, safety and welfare to make a quick buck. On television and in the movies, business executives increasingly became villains, to be challenged by heroic lawyers, policemen, reporters and activists.

By the 1970s, the multinational had become synonymous, around the world, with power and wealth and, to many, a potent symbol of the economic and political dominance of the USA. What is striking about much of the literature on multinationals from that time, compared with today, is the extent to which the interests of the multinational are identified with the interests of its state of origin, or 'home state'. Multinationals were viewed, perhaps simplistically, as economic agents of their home states, with no particular allegiances to the states in which they chose to invest. With this mindset, the nationality of the foreign investor was of crucial importance. Foreign-owned multinationals were regarded as a threat to the sovereignty of their host states in two ways: first, because of fears that they might exercise undue influence over the host state's national policies and, second, because they helped to perpetuate inequalities between states. But while foreign ownership of local industry was a concern for all host states, these issues had particular significance for less developed countries.

Legal Jurisdiction Of Multinationals

Multinationals are not traditional subjects of international law. Historically, the role of international law in relation to multinationals has primarily been to define the rights and obligations of states with respect to international investment issues. International law has been used to regulate the jurisdiction of states over multinationals, and their rights of diplomatic protection and, through treaties, has provided states with a means by which investment conditions for multinationals could be stabilised, harmonised, and generally enhanced.

But the world is changing fast. Concern about the social and environmental impacts of 'globalisation' means that new demands are now being made of international law. Can international law respond to these demands? Does international law provide an adequate framework for the regulation of the social and environmental impacts of multinationals on a global scale? Many people think not. Some have doubted that international law is even 'conceptually equipped' to perform such a role.

Public opinion, too, is generally sceptical as to the extent to which multinationals can be regulated effectively. Critics point out the ease with which multinationals can avoid national regulation through their mobility and flexibility of structure and organisation. While each state is entitled to regulate those parts of a multinational incorporated or operating within its territory, many states may not have the resources or political will to do so effectively, giving rise to differences in social and environmental standards between states. These differences, it is argued, are exploited by some multinationals for commercial advantage; that is, multinationals will tend to gravitate to regions in which production costs are lowest because of low regulatory standards and expectations.

Reference

Hessen, Robert (2008). "Corporations". In David R. Henderson. Concise Encyclopedia of Economics. Indianapolis: Library of Economics and Liberty.

Low, Albert, 2008. "Conflict and Creativity at Work: Human Roots of Corporate Life, Sussex Academic Press.

RR Formoy, The Historical Foundations of Company Law (Sweet and Maxwell 1923)

P Frentrop, A History of Corporate Governance 1602–2002 (Brussels et al., 2003)

J Micklethwait and A Wooldridge, The company: A short history of a revolutionary idea (Modern Library 2003)

Hunt, Bishop. The Development of the Business Corporation in England (1936)

Davis, Joseph S. Essays in the Earlier History of American Corporations (1917)

Dynamics Of World Hunger

A recent article in The Nation, titled "Manufacturing a Food Crisis", by Walden Bello, explains much of the dynamics of world hunger in today's world:

The apostles of the free market and the defenders of dumping - the policies they advocate are bringing about a globalized capitalist industrial agriculture. Developing countries are being integrated into a system where export-oriented production of meat and grain is dominated by large industrial farms. The elimination of tariff and nontariff barriers is facilitating a global agricultural supermarket of elite and middle-class consumers.

There is little room for the hundreds of millions of rural and urban poor in this integrated global market. They are confined to giant suburban slums, where they contend with high food prices or to rural reservations, where they are trapped in marginal agricultural activities and increasingly vulnerable to hunger. Indeed, within the same country, famine in the marginalized sector sometimes coexists with prosperity in the globalized sector.

This transformation is a traumatic one for hundreds of millions of people, since *peasant production is not simply an economic activity. It is an ancient way of life, a culture.*

Such is, and has always been, the results of imperialism – war, misery, and the repression of the many, so that a small minority may live in luxury beyond the imagination of most normal people.

Rush To Control

The Third World's Food Supply

A disturbing trend in the food sector is accelerating worldwide with the emergence of the new "food barons". There is no better way to control a country than to control its food supply.

Indian government is brazenly siding with these demoniac forces and putting the country's food supply up for grabs. Following reports may testify to this fact.

Clinton Gives GM Crops A Push

Though Hillary Avoided The Emotive Word GM, She Waxed Eloquent On Agri Tech
Rumu Banerjee | Times of India, Jul 20, 2009

New Delhi: Days after the government said it was planning to introduce genetically modified food crops in the country in three years, US secretary of state Hillary Clinton gave a clear indication of the US administration's approval of deploying 'cutting-edge technology' to raise crop yields.

During her first visit to India as secretary of state, which included a strategic stop at the country's premier agriculture institute, Indian Agricultural Research Institute, Clinton was vocal about the need to address the "root" of the problem of world hunger: Crop productivity. And helping increase crop yield would be cutting-edge technology, she claimed.

"India's leadership in agriculture is absolutely crucial,"Clinton said as she spoke at length on the US administration's focus on global hunger and malnutrition. Pledging to "work and support" Indian initiatives, Clinton added,"We have to work together. It is imperative that we invest in science that increases crop yield."

The remarks comes in the face of continued opposition to genetically modified food crops in India.

Clinton's statement at the Pusa institute, however, was clear about where the US administration stood on the issue. Talking about the Green Revolution that took place in India in the 1960s, she emphasized the need for close cooperation between the two countries again: This time, in agriculture and the use of technology in this field.

Food For Thought: Agriculture minister Sharad Pawar with US Secretary of State Hillary Clinton at IARI in New Delhi

"India has 3% of the world's crop land but feeds 17% of the world's population. Its leadership in agriculture is crucial... we are looking at ways to accelerate in a short period of time the growth of productivity," Clinton said.

Asked about the US's commitment to GM crops, as opposed to the cautious stand taken by the EU, Clinton admitted,"We're looking at it in a holistic way, by being very vigilant about how we do it. "Interestingly, while the emphasis on technology in agriculture was more than apparent, Clinton avoided using the emotive word 'GM' throughout.

However, Clinton's visit -- which was to learn more about research done by IARI, helped by US funding, to develop seeds that give better productivity and crops that use less water as well as farm equipment that reduce production costs -- was indicative of the thrust on technology that US plans to give in the collaboration agreement that will be signed on Monday.

Speaking about the "five pillars of collaboration that India and US would be redefining", Clinton said agriculture was one of the "strongest pillars". Giving support to Clinton's statement was agriculture minister Sharad Pawar. "For India,a key priority is to trigger the next generation of reforms in the agrarian economy ... Our joint collaboration in frontier areas of research including biotechnology could make a significant contribution to the world," he said.

Accompanying Clinton was new US ambassador to India Timothy Roemer and special envoy on climate change Todd Stern as well as other senior officials. Also present were Dr Mangala Rai,DG,ICAR; Indian ambassador to US Meera Shankar, A K Upadhyay, special secretary, department of agriculture and education and H S Gupta, director, IARI.

Agriculture To Be Pillar Of Us-India Cooperation: Clinton

Zeenews, July 19, 2009

New Delhi: Stating that India was well positioned to help it lead the fight against hunger, the US on Sunday said agriculture will be the strongest of the five pillars of cooperation the Obama administration was seeking with New Delhi.

"We will be announcing the five pillars of our cooperation (after talks tomorrow). And one of the strongest and most important will be agriculture,"US Secretary of State Hillary Clinton told reporters

---

Government Of The Criminals, By The Criminals, For The Criminals Latest reports (2012) state that 162 members of parliament in India (out of 545) have legal charges levied against them and are being investigated. There is a high level of criminalization in politics, which is now getting regularly exposed. A number of members of parliament were implicated in scams last year. This has put the government on a back foot and political parties are losing ground. In nutshell, Indian politics is tough and dirty.

after a visit to the Indian Agriculture Research Institute (IARI), where she toured the agriculture research site.

Recalling 50 years of US-Indo partnership in agriculture, Clinton said, "We have to work together because it is imperative that we invest in science that will increase crop yields."

"We have collaborated over more than 50 years and today we called to collaborate once again," she said.

Areas of collaboration she highlighted included linking farms and markets so that farmers can sell their products, expanding the export of technology and training to bring more assistance to farmers, and strengthening the response to climate change, which threatens the waterways that sustain agriculture in many parts of the world including South Asia.

Stating that hunger persists and affects the entire human conditions as well as peace, she said, "It would be a signature issue of the Obama administration to do what we can to fight hunger

The so-called political leaders are busy making plans to advance the material prosperity of their nation, but factually these political leaders only want an exalted position for themselves. Due to their greed for material position, they falsely present themselves as leaders before the people and collect their votes, although they are completely under the grip of the laws of material nature. These are some of the faults of modern civilization. Without taking to God consciousness and accepting the authority of the Lord, the living entities become ultimately confused and frustrated in their planmaking attempts. Due to their unauthorized plans for economic development, the price of commodities is rising daily all over the world, so much so that is has become difficult for the poorer classes, and they are suffering the consequences. And due to lack of Krsna consciousness, people are being fooled by so-called leaders and planmakers. Consequently, the sufferings of the people are increasing. According to the laws of nature, which are backed by the Lord, nothing can be permanent within this material world; therefore everyone should be allowed to take shelter of the Absolute in order to be saved.

~ Srila Prabhupada (Srimad Bhagavatam 4.24.66)

and extend food security. And India is well positioned to help us lead this fight."

"The work has already begun clearly here, when I just saw scientists are developing seeds that produce higher yields, crops that require less water, farm equipment that conserve energy. All this is part of meeting the challenge we face with global hunger," she said.

On possible areas of partnerships, Clinton said the two nations are working together to produce better seeds, hybrids that can grow with less water and new farming techniques.

"We have no limits on what we are going to be exploring together. But our goal is the same -- we want to improve agriculture productivity. We want to get more of agriculture dollar into the hands of the farmer. We want India to do more food processing and value added agriculture.

"We are going to be working with India very closely. And I am excited about the potential that holds," she said.

"So as we look at strengthening agriculture and fighting hunger particularly in South Asia, but also in Africa and elsewhere, India's leadership is absolutely crucial. And the United States is today just as proud to work with and support India's efforts as we were 50 years ago," Clinton said.

Stating that the world has the resources to feed everyone, Clinton said, "Nonetheless, hunger persists; that is why the G-8 and other countries committed USD 20 billion to end global hunger." The US has committed USD 3.5 billion to this effort. Clinton noted that research is a critical component in improving agriculture.

14

Too Powerful

For Being Just A Firm

Of the world's 100 largest economic entities, 51 are multinational companies and 49 are nation states. Sales and net profit figures for some multinationals are higher than GNPs of developing countries, like for example the annual sales of Shell are roughly £68billion, which is two and half times the income of Nigeria's 110 million people. In 1989, more than 18 per cent of all share trading was in the shares of the major multinationals.

In 1993 the combined assets of the top 300 MNCs would make up roughly a quarter of the worlds $20trillion productive assets and there was an accusation by Jack Behrman that several American companies could "buy out" some European countries. Coca-Cola advertisements are being shown 560 million times a day, everyday in 160 countries, while majority of world population does not know where Fiji is.

These facts and figures undoubtfully may lead to the conclusion that indeed the MNCs do possess distinctive economical superiority over some nation states, and therefore are too powerful for being

Since MNCs dominate media production and distribution – just six corporations sell 80 percent of all the recorded music worldwide – they introduce ideas and images that some governments and religious groups fear may destabilize their societies.

just a firm with such cynical target as profit maximisation and not welfare of the citizens.

Accelerated process of Globalisation is one of the main features of twentieth century world politics and is "one of the most dramatic developments of the period and has more than just economical and industrial significance". Professor Sakamoto has identified the globalisation of capitalism as the "…key element in the changing world order". Accordingly, the notion of the nation state becomes less vivid, while new actors, such as multinational companies are being spotted on the international stage. Multinationals(MNCs) by their virtue are direct creations of globalisation, however, the humanity is still in doubt whether the sudden "mushrooming" of these institutions bodes good for the new global order or whether they are going to turn into 'mutant monsters' causing major economic disasters. Bill Emott argued that Multinationals do not dominate the world market and 'are not even global', while others strongly feel that "multinationals are increasingly going global" and call them "powerful beasts".

> *"Human prosperity flourishes by natural gifts and not by gigantic industrial enterprises. The gigantic industrial enterprises are products of a godless civilization, and they cause the destruction of the noble aims of human life. The more we go on increasing such troublesome industries to squeeze out the vital energy of the human being, the more there will be unrest and dissatisfaction of the people in general, although a few only can live lavishly by exploitation. The natural gifts such as grains and vegetables, fruits, rivers, the hills of jewels and minerals, and the seas full of pearls are supplied by the order of the Supreme, and as He desires, material nature produces them in abundance or restricts them at times."*
> *-Srila Prabhupada (Srimad Bhagavatam 1.8.40)*

MNCs have emerged because of 'structural' and 'inherent' market imperfections, such as restrictions on imports, excise duties, subsidies, unstable exchange rates, distribution and marketing costs and have grown rapidly because of economies of scale and particularly due to their burst through national boundaries, customs and ideologies.

The primary target of promotional policies of multinationals is to create one customer culture, so that people around the globe purchase identical basket of goods: "watch Hollywood films on Phillips television set, while smoking Marlboro and drinking Coke". During the 1970s largest number out of 7000 MNCs was based in USA. By the early 1990s there were 35000 multinationals, however USA still maintained its leadership. These companies aim at promoting same goods around the globe in order to create one identical consumer culture, which is very much influenced by that of American.

Historically, public opposition to multinationals has arisen mainly from concerns about undue concentrations of power, and their implications for national sovereignty and cultures. In recent years, however, there has been a shift in emphasis away from these 'state-centred' concerns towards more 'people-centred' concerns, such as the environment and human rights.

Reference

Phillip I. Blumberg, The Multinational Challenge to Corporation Law: The Search for a New Corporate Personality, (1993)

Galbraith, J.K. 1967, The new industrial state, Houghton Mifflin, Boston.

Hawken, P., Lovins, A.B. & Lovins, L.H. 1999, Natural capitalism: creating the next industrial revolution, 1st edn, Little, Brown and Co., Boston.

"The dinosaur's eloquent lesson is that if some bigness is good, an overabundance of bigness is not necessarily better."
- Eric Johnston.

15

Profit

The Only Thing That Matters

A corporation has its own life; it lives for profit, at all costs. It only shares humane concerns for social and environmental issues insofar as it is profitable to do so. Actions deemed to be cooperative with environmental, health, safety or social concerns, are motivated primarily by self interest, the wider interests of society are a distant second. Legally there is nothing wrong with this; it is what a corporation is designed to do, and what it is bound by through its charter. As such we should not expect anything more from these profit making economic entities, and we should certainly not expect them to harbour any significant environmental or social concern.

A profit oriented private enterprise can never look after the citizens' welfare the way a government can. For example, crop insurance is not an area where any private insurance company would be interested, but the government can go beyond the concern for profitability in the insurance business and subsidise crop insurance in order to stabilise agricultural earnings and make investment in agriculture less risky and more attractive.

Similarly, no private electricity company would be even remotely interested in distributing power to widely diffused rural settlements. This is a task that only a state enterprise would undertake, maybe at a loss initially, and with a generous subsidy; but if it helps the local economy to bloom, maybe in the long run, it will help make profit. There is also the question of the interests of future generations. A private company motivated only by profit and discounting the present value of future earnings at the current rate of interest, would not see anything beyond 15 years, as the present value of earnings beyond that period would be nearly zero. Only the government can protect the interests of future generations and save the environment from degradation that is not discernible at one point of time but accumulates over decades - for example, the depletion of the ozone shield.

For a corporation, environmental concerns are secondary to securing profit, and environmental catastrophes are common

santustasya nirihasya
svatmaramasya yat sukham
kutas tat kama-lobhena
dhavato 'rthehaya disah
One who is content and satisfied and who links his activities with the Supreme Personality of Godhead residing in everyone's heart enjoys transcendental happiness without endeavoring for his livelihood. Where is such happiness for a materialistic man who is impelled by lust and greed and who therefore wanders in all directions with a desire to accumulate wealth?
sada santusta-manasah
sarvah sivamaya disah
sarkara-kantakadibhyo
yathopanat-padah sivam
For a person who has suitable shoes on his feet, there is no danger even when he walks on pebbles and thorns. For him, everything is auspicious. Similarly, for one who is always self-satisfied there is no distress; indeed, he feels happiness everywhere.
~ Srila Prabhupada (Srimad Bhagavatam 7.15.16-17)

'externalities' of the business economy. At a time when many of our resources are depleting globally- in particular our fossil fuels, and even regionally-such as water supplies, the profit motive does not encourage restraint or conservation. Logically, a profit making company cannot advise its customers to consume less, as this directly undermines business revenues. In the case of fossil fuels, this simple fact has seen the continual increase in oil consumption that is so dangerously poisoning our biosphere. It is unlikely that alternative energy production will prove more profitable in the near future, and thus quite unlikely that alternatives will be vigorously pursued by profit making companies.

In the UK, despite current drought conditions and water usage restrictions imposed upon the general public, Thames Water PLC has declared record pre-tax profits. Meanwhile it has neglected to reduce the 894 million litres a day that is lost through faulty pipes and leakage. A publicly owned and managed water supplier would not be under financial pressure by shareholders and would be able to reinvest profits into infrastructure and conservation.

Reference

Korten, D.C. 1995, When corporations rule the world, Kumarian Press; Berrett-Koehler Publishers

Litvin, D.B. 2003, Empires of profit: commerce, conquest and corporate responsibility, Texere, New York.

Jacoby, N.H. 1973, Corporate power and social responsibility; a blueprint for the future, Macmillan, New York.

16

Return of

Barbaric Slave Trade

Call Centre Workers Limited To Eight Minutes Toilet Time Per Day... And Risk Triggering Alarm If They Go One Second Over

Call centre workers in Norway are protesting against a high-tech surveillance system that triggers an alarm if they spend more than eight minutes per day in the toilet.

Managers are alerted by flashing lights if an employee is away from their desk for a toilet break or other 'personal activities' beyond the allocated time.

But unions and workplace inspectors have branded the practice at insurance company DNB as 'highly intrusive' and a potential breach of their human rights.

Norway's privacy regulator Datatilsynet has now written to DNB telling them the monitoring system is 'a major violation of privacy'.

It said: 'Each individual worker has different needs and these kinds of strict controls deprive the employees of all freedoms over the course of their working day.'

The employees union Finansforbundet described the rules as unacceptable.

A spokesman added: 'Surveying staff to limit toilet visits, cigarette breaks, personal phone calls and other other personal needs to a total of eight minutes per day is highly restrictive and intrusive and must be stopped.'

Previously in Norway a company ordered all female staff to wear red bracelets during their periods

It is the latest example of 'tyrannical' toilet rules in Norwegian companies.

Last year the country's workplace ombudsman said one firm was reported for making women workers wear a red bracelet when they were having their period to justify more frequent trips to the toilet.

Another company made staff sign a toilet 'visitors book' while a third issued employees with an electronic key card to gain access to the toilets so they could monitor breaks.

Norway's chief workplace ombudsman Bjorn Erik Thon said: 'These are extreme cases of workplace monitoring, but they are real.

'Toilet Codes relating to menstrual cycles are clear violations of privacy and is very insulting to the people concerned.

'We receive many complaints about monitoring in the workplace, which is becoming a growing problem as it is so often being used for something other than what it was originally intended for.

'Wear A Sign When You Want To Use Toilet'

A Spanish factory boss ordered female workers to wear a red sign around their necks when they wanted to use the toilet.

Just like here you see in Europe, America. They have got the high standard of life, they have got skyscraper buildings, very big, big roads, motorcars. But what is that? Simply struggling. Are they happy?
—*Srila Prabhupada (Lecture, Srimad-Bhagavatam, Vrndavana, December 7, 1975)*

The 400 women staff were told to wear the sign with the word 'aseo' - Spanish for lavatory - written on it in a bid to humiliate them into taking fewer loo-breaks.

Employees at the El Ciruelo fruit packing plant in Murcia even began drinking less water in stifling heat to put off using the toilets.

Humiliating: A female member staff at the Spanish fruit company El Ciruelo in Murcia is shown wearing a sign that reads 'toilet'

This Post Received Thousands Of Comments Which Describe Similar Conditions Prevailing In Other Work Places

This is not a unique situation but a general trend in work places. Some of these comments are reproduced below which confirm the horrors of modern work places.

Remember you are no longer human beings in this world, you are a resource, just like steel, paper, packaging etc. The euphoria of the seventies and the growth of societies that allowed human beings to enjoy life, work and leisure, was swallowed by the accountants and reduced to numbers on a chart

- Andy, Derby, 2/2/2012

Vodafone inbound directory enquiries - 2 minutes toilet break, any longer and you had to explain to manager exactly why. I was very ill following a miscarriage and the manager came looking for me to see why I'd been over 2 minutes. Human rights? Pah!

- Mamastar, 1/2/2012

British Airways call centre, Manchester.. It's a "Bio-break" there with the managers screens going red after 7 minutes absence during the course of the day! Worst job I ever had.

- JoeyR, Leeds, Manchester UK, 1/2/2012

And how much loyalty can you expect slaves to show to their masters? Just a thought...

- DrMallard, West Palm Beach, Florida, USA, 1/2/2012

I worked in a call centre for a while and they tried to stop me from going to the loo one day.......I said "That's fine..no problem at all" then I just ended up peeing on the floor when finally couldn't control...
- Sara, London, 1/2/2012

This type of employer restriction used to be against the law. A deliberate policy to restrict the natural needs of workers. What a nasty sweat shop of a country we have become.
- Sylvia, Northumberland, 1/2/2012

Working for a company doing inbound directory Enquiries, we had to complete each call within 25 secs and as soon as you got off one call within 1 second you was on the next call, all time was monitored, including toilet breaks. At the end of my shift I had fried brains. Now the government want to put sick people into these kinds of stressful jobs.
- John.mitch, Belfast, 1/2/2012

This is what happens when profit is put before people and an organisation is run by anti-humans, obsessed with targets and costs. How desperately sad, but everyone in the know knows this kind of thing is normal in the UK too. Maybe not the red bracelets though...yet.
- Deborah, 1/2/2012

I fail to see how this is breaking news. Egg bank were doing this 10 years ago!!
- Julie Watts, Derby, UK, 1/2/2012

Working in a call centre is a fast track to mental illness. Ask anyone who has worked in one.
- Richard, Yorkshire, 1/2/2012

I've worked at call centres for BT, and for a major software company. Both did the same thing - if you wanted to go to the toilet, you were given a code which you had to put in your phone, and if you went over

your allotted time your manager wanted to know why. Worse, at the software company a report went to the whole team each day so that each person could 'see where they went wrong' and coincidentally also see how much time their colleagues spent on the toilet...
   - Christy Andersen, Newcastle, UK, 1/2/2012

Its not unique to Norway. Lets concentrate on our own country!
   - Cat, Midlands, 1/2/2012

And we criticize the Chinese how absolutely hypercritical can you get? - Carl Barron, Christchurch, Dorset,

So too bad for people who suffer from IBS or some other gastrointestinal complaint! too bad for the women who have to visit the loo at that time of the month! too bad for the worker with gas buildup...guess the co-workers will just have to put up with the smell! Honestly, people are not treated as a human these days! Workers are adults, who should be able to determine what amount of time and frequency they need to attend to normal bodily functions. Just typing this, i think i have passed wind at least 5 times and made one trip to the loo for no 1's...if i was working in that company, i guess i wouldn't be too popular tonight!
   - Blondie, Wales, 1/2/2012

Same thing happens within BT Openreach repair centres......
   - Matt Munro, Bristol, UK, 1/2/2012

I used to work in a a large mail order company, they were the same, however there was no union so they got away with it... It's shocking really, we should name and shame... Next.
   - Laura, Oz, 1/2/2012

What are you supposed to do if you have a dose of diarrhoea?
   - Honest joe, 1/2/2012

This is why I quit my job in a call centre. It was incredibly stressful. The more recent one I tried was very difficult for me. I found that with the constant talking, my mouth got incredibly dry, hence the need to drink more, hence the need to go to the loo more. I have made a clear decision that this is not the right work environment for me. I did not enjoy being treated as a recalcitrant child. I used to go home depressed at the end of the day. I was consumed by this job and it was so draining. Well the supervisor rang me up to ask me why I was not taking any calls. I am currently upskilling so that I can make a change into something more appropriate.

- RLH, Sydney, Australia, 1/2/2012

When I worked at NHS Direct we were monitored similarly. Needless to say a lot of us left.

- Chloe, UK, 1/2/2012

I wonder does that include travelling time to and from the toilet?

- Paul, Surrey, 1/2/2012

Every night I still hear my former team leader shout that dreaded phrase .... CALLS WAITING!!!

- Dagenham Dave, London, 1/2/2012 0:38

Errr...since when is this news??? I work in a call centre for a major bank, in an eight hour shift we are allowed 14 minutes 'productivity' time. We can split this up during the day for loo breaks, getting a drink etc. But if we are even a few seconds over it, the next day you get an interrogation from your manager and have to explain why you are over the time. I am in mid 30s and have two children and don't mind saying that I need to p** at least a few times a day! Come 5pm I am literally running out the door before I explode =(And its hard enough when every single customer thinks It's my personal fault that the tax payer had to bail us out and that our chief exec gets a bazillion pound bonus! The abuse is unbelieveable at times. Anyway, needs must, bills have to get paid so I put up with it and dream of the day when I can finally tell them to shove it. Now where did I put that lottery ticket..........

- Jena, Glasgow, 1/2/2012

I worked in a call centre. On my break on my last day I went out and bought cakes for everyone and was 5 minutes late back from my break (in my 2 years there, my time keeping was impeccable). During my exit interview held 1 hour before I left for the last time ever, the manager gave me a warning because I had been late from my break!! I promised her I wouldn't do it again....

- - Al, Warrington, 1/2/2012

About forty years ago I was working as a storeman in a paintbrush factory, I received an emergency call from a hospital saying my grandmother was close to death, I was told I could not leave until a workmate returned from a dental appointment. I was told that if I left before this I would have no job to return to, I finally got to the hospital less than half an hour before my grandmother died.

- Nick M, Birmingham UK, 1/2/2012

In this country NHS Direct call handlers and nurses have been monitored on toilet (comfort) breaks for years.

- Gideon Webley, Wakefield, 31/1/2012

I saw workers being treated in a very similar way back in England when I was working at an award winning international company. It's not just call centres though - as a student I worked in a major high street department store. You were expected not to go to the bathroom or have a drink during a 4 hour shift chunk. Not very handy for certain times of the month!! If you did need to go, you had to find the head of department and get permission like a school kid, and it was marked down like a crime in 'the book'! It was a huge store with loads of staff per department so it wasn't like it caused a problem.

- JJ, expat, Canada (will return when the government represents its people), 31/1/2012

"Innocent men, women, they are kept in that factory simply for livelihood. A little work will provide their needs. Nature has given so much facility. They can grow a little food anywhere. The cows are there in the pasturing ground. Take milk and live peacefully. Why you open factories?"

— Srila Prabhupada (New Vrindavan, June 26, 1976)

Try having IBS mate, you can be on the toilet for 30 mins in excruciating pain being literally held hostage by your bowels when all you want is to have a normal working day. I have worked in a sompany and they made you press a 'time out' button on your computer which flashed up a big timer to show how long you'd been away from your desk (which the supervisors would come and check). It's humiliating and embarrassing, people shouldn't be punished for things they can't help and have no control over, especially when there's no cure! These places are the pits, and it's bad enough for people who have normal bodily processes. Since leaving (fortunately just paying my way through university) I know how mind numbing and horrible it is to work in them!

- Marcus, London, 31/1/2012

Source
Ian Sparks, The Daily Mail, 31 January 2012
http://www.labourstart.org/2013
Where Is Everyone? Attrition Rates In Call Centres, August 31, 2013, The Secret Diary of A Call Centre

17

Countries On Sale

Companies Are Buying Off The Third World

The 'Neo-Colonial' Food Grab

In the 1800s, European colonial powers divided up the Third World in their quest for primary agricultural and mineral commodities. In post-colonial times, oil corporations have gained oil concessions in these nations through questionable dealings with local elites, enriching the elites and leaving the vast majority in these countries desperately poor. Recently, a new scramble has begun: the attempt by food-deficit countries, primarily in the Middle East, to buy or rent hundreds of thousands of hectares of prime agricultural land in the poor countries. In the meantime, millions in these countries are starving and are in desperate need of food aid.

What is spurring this attempt to secure agricultural land in other countries is the global food crisis and price volatility. Saudi Arabia and other oil exporting Middle Eastern countries have decided to use their oil wealth to buy land in poorer nations, including Ukraine, Kazakhstan, Pakistan, Uganda, Ethiopia and Sudan. China is also trying to buy lands abroad, but is concentrating on Kazakhstan.

In August, Andrew England reported in The Financial Times that "Saudi Arabia plans to set up large-scale projects overseas that will later involve the private sector in growing crops such as corn, wheat and rice. Once a country has been selected, each project could be in excess of 100,000 hectares – about ten times the size of Manhattan Island – and the majority of the crop would be exported directly to Saudi Arabia. This is not trade, but direct shipment of food crops to the land-owners.

"While Saudi Arabia's plans are among the grandest, they reflect growing interest in such projects among capital-rich countries that import most of their food. The United Arab Emirates is looking into Kazakhstan and Sudan. Libya is hoping to lease farms in Ukraine, and South Korea has hinted at plans in Mongolia."

Joachim von Braun, director of the International Food Policy Research Institute, says, "This is a new trend within the global food crisis. The dominant force today is security of food supplies."

England wrote, "Alarmed by exporting countries' trade restrictions – such as India's curbs on exports of rice, Ukraine's halt to wheat shipments, and Argentina's imposition of heavy taxes on overseas sales of soya – importing countries have realized that their dependence on the international food market makes them vulnerable not only to an abrupt surge in prices but, more crucially, to an interruption in supplies. As a result, food security is at the top of the political agenda for the first time since the 1970s."

For poor countries rich in cultivable land and water but short of capital, such plans could also make a lot of sense. Lennart Bage, of the UN's International Fund for Agriculture Development in Rome, says that "land was long thought less important than oil or mineral deposits. But now fertile land with access to water has become a strategic asset."

Sudan is seeking to attract at least one billion dollars of capital for its agricultural sector from Arab and Asian investment groups.

Jacques Diouf, director general of the U.N. Food and Agriculture Organization, has warned that the headlong drive by rich food-importing countries to buy up vast tracts of farmland in the world's poorer states risks "creating a neo-colonial" agricultural system.

The investment ministry is marketing 17 large-scale projects that would cover an area of 880,000 hectares.

Ethiopia's Prime Minister Meles Zenawi is also enthusiastic. He welcomed the Saudi agriculture delegation with the following words: "We would be very eager to provide hundreds of thousands of hectares of agricultural land for investment."

The food-producing countries need to be wary of these deals, warns England. "Through secretive bilateral agreements, the investors hope to be able to bypass any potential trade restriction that the host country might impose during a crisis."

Maryknoll Father Ken Thesing, who is working with the Jesuit Refugee Service in Juba, Southern Sudan, offers further insight and caution, "In Southern Sudan we have vast tracts of land that can be very productive, without irrigation. But we need infrastructure, inputs, and expertise to positively 'harvest' the potential of the land. It is going to be a challenge to do that without Southern Sudan ending up either missing the opportunity to move ahead and use its natural advantage at this time of food shortage/crisis or ending up exploited by other 'rich' countries and entrepreneurs using the resources for their private benefit."

Lennart Bage, president of the U.N. International Fund for Agriculture Development in Rome, says that land was long considered less important than oil or mineral resources.

But now, with food prices having doubled on average from a year ago, "fertile land with access to water has become a strategic asset."

But many of the countries whose farmland is being snapped up are already unable to feed their own people, and it may be just a matter of time before that triggers anti-government unrest and the resource wars that many fear will erupt in the coming decades.

For some policymakers this evokes the nightmare scenario of crops being transported out of fortified farms as hungry locals look on. Jacques Diouf, director general of the UN Food and Agriculture Organization (FAO), says he dreads "the emergence of a neocolonial pact for the supply of raw materials with no value added for the producer countries. We are deliberating on land policy tools that we can use to counsel the governments involved. The idea is not to renounce such a potential godsend, but to avoid expropriations of small producers and speculation."

Alain Karsenty, a researcher in agronomics, claims that there will be another devastating impact of the headlong rush into these agricultural schemes – deforestation. "As the price of agricultural land increases, land with forest values will lose profitability. Maintaining forests, whether for environmental purposes or for economic purposes, will be abandoned as a national objective."

In his new book, Rising Powers, Shrinking Planet: The New Geopolitics of Energy, Michael T. Klare writes that we are now seeing the resurrection of a mercantilist form of global economy, similar to the colonial era of the 19th century, when national states took control of resources in colonial territories. As essential to the global economy as are corporations, the effort to lock in foreign sources of energy and strategic resources is now "statist," rather than corporate. Examples in the energy sector are President Bush's two trips to Saudi Arabia to plead for increased oil production in order to stabilize prices, and China's dealings with Sudan (also Congo and Zimbabwe).

These state efforts to insure that energy, strategic metals and food will go to rich countries is further marginalizing the poor countries, where many of these resources are found. To sum up his analysis: the first quarter of the 21st century is characterized by a statist effort to lock in foreign sources of strategic resources, in a planet now running out of these resources, increasing the possibility of military confrontations between nuclear powers.

George Monbiot of the Guardian concludes with this harsh outlook. "None of this is to suggest that the poor nations should not sell food to the rich. To escape from famine, countries must enhance their purchasing power. This often means selling farm products and increasing their value by processing them locally. But there is nothing fair about the deals described above. Where once they used gunboats and sepoys, the rich nations now use checkbooks and lawyers to seize food from the hungry. The scramble for resources has begun, but in the short term, at any rate, we will hardly notice. The rich world's governments will protect themselves from the political cost of shortages, even if it means that other people must starve."

In 2008, the South Korean multinational Daewoo Logistics secured 1.3 million hectares of farmland in Madagascar, half the size of Belgium, to grow maize and crops for biofuels. Roughly half of the country's arable land, as well as rainforests of rich and unique biodiversity, were to be converted into palm and corn monocultures, producing food for export from a country where a third of the population and 50 percent of children under 5 are malnourished, using workers imported from South Africa instead of locals. Those living on the land were never consulted or informed, despite being dependent on the land for food and income. The controversial deal played a major part in prolonged anti-government protests on the island that resulted in over a hundred deaths. Shortly after the Madagascar deal, Tanzania announced that South Korea was in talks to develop 100,000 hectares for food production and processing for 700 to 800 billion won. Scheduled to be completed in 2010, it will be the largest single piece of agricultural infrastructure South Korea has ever built overseas.

In 2009, Hyundai Heavy Industries acquired a majority stake in a company cultivating 10,000 hectares of farmland in the Russian Far East and a wealthy South Korean provincial government secured 95,000 hectares of farmland in Oriental Mindoro, central Philippines, to grow corn. The South Jeolla province became the first provincial government to benefit from a newly created central government fund to develop farmland overseas, receiving a cheap loan of $1.9 million for the Mindoro project. The feedstock is expected to produce 10,000 tonnes of feed in the first year for South Korea. South Korean multinationals and provincial governments have also purchased land in Sulawesi, Indonesia, Cambodia and Bulgan, Mongolia. The South Korean government itself announced its intention to invest 30 billion won in land in Paraguay and Uruguay. Discussions with Laos, Myanmar and Senegal are also currently underway.

Source:
NewsNotes, November–December 2008
Pedersen, E.R. & Huniche, M. (eds) 2006, Corporate Citizenship in Developing Countries: New Partnership Perspectives, Copenhagen Business School Press, Copenhagen.

18

Banana Slavery

And Banana Massacres

A Fruit That Changed The World

The United Fruit Company was an American corporation that traded in tropical fruit (primarily bananas) grown on Central and South American plantations and sold in the United States and Europe. The company was formed in 1899.

It flourished in the early and mid-20th century and came to control vast territories and transportation networks in Central America, the Caribbean coast of Colombia, Ecuador, and the West Indies. Though it competed with the Standard Fruit Company for dominance in the international banana trade, it maintained a virtual monopoly in certain regions, some of which came to be called banana republics.

It had a deep and long-lasting impact on the economic and political development of several Latin American countries. Critics often accused it of exploitative neocolonialism and described it as the archetypal example of the influence of a multinational corporation on the internal politics of the banana republics.

At its founding in 1899, United Fruit was capitalized at US$11,230,000. The company proceeded to buy a share in 14 competitors, assuring them of 80% of the banana import business in the United States, then their main source of income.

In 1901, the government of Guatemala hired the United Fruit Company to manage the country's postal service and in 1913 the United Fruit Company created the Tropical Radio and Telegraph Company. By 1930 it had absorbed more than 20 rival firms, acquiring a capital of US$215,000,000 and becoming the largest employer in Central America.

Throughout most of its history, United Fruit's main competitor was the Standard Fruit Company, now the Dole Food Company.

Reputation

The United Fruit Company was frequently accused of bribing government officials in exchange for preferential treatment, exploiting its workers, paying little by way of taxes to the governments of the countries in which it operated, and working ruthlessly to consolidate monopolies. Latin American journalists sometimes referred to the company as el pulpo ("the octopus"), and leftist parties in Central and South America encouraged the company's workers to strike.

Criticism of the United Fruit Company became a staple of the discourse of the communist parties in several Latin American countries, where its activities were often interpreted as illustrating Vladimir Lenin's theory of capitalist imperialism. Major left-wing writers in Latin America, such as Carlos Luis Fallas of Costa Rica, Ramón Amaya Amador of Honduras, Miguel Ángel Asturias and Augusto Monterroso of Guatemala, Gabriel García Márquez of Colombia, and Pablo Neruda of Chile, denounced the company in their literature.

The business practices of United Fruit were also frequently criticized by journalists, politicians, and artists in the United States. Little Steven released a song called "Bitter Fruit" in 1987 in which lyrics referred to a hard life for a company "far away" and whose accompanying video, depicted orange groves worked by peasants overseen by wealthy managers. Although the lyrics and scenery are generic, United Fruit (or its successor Chiquita) was reputed to be the target. In 1950, Gore Vidal published a novel "Dark Green, Bright Red", in which a thinly fictionalized version of United Fruit supports a military coup in a thinly fictionalized Guatemala.

History in Central America

The United Fruit Company (UFCO) owned vast tracts of land in the Caribbean lowlands. UFCO's policies of acquiring tax breaks and other benefits from host governments led to it building enclave economies in the regions, in which a company's investment is largely self-contained for its employees and overseas investors and the benefits of the export earnings are not shared with the host country.

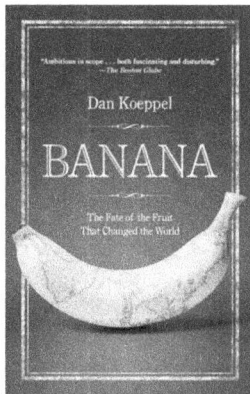

One of the company's primary tactics for maintaining market dominance was to control the distribution of banana lands. UFCO claimed that hurricanes, blight and other natural threats required them to hold extra land or reserve land. In practice, what this meant was that UFCO was able to prevent the government from distributing banana lands to peasants who wanted a share of the banana trade.

The fact that the UFCO relied so heavily on manipulation of land use rights in order to maintain their market dominance had a number of long-term consequences for the region. For the company to maintain its unequal land holdings it often required government concessions. And this in turn meant that the company had to be politically involved in the region even though it was an American company. In fact, the heavy-handed involvement of the company in governments which often were or became corrupt created the term "Banana republic" representing a "servile dictatorship".

It allowed vast tracts of land under its ownership to remain uncultivated and, in Guatemala and elsewhere, it discouraged the government from building highways, which would lessen the profitable transportation monopoly of the railroads under its control. UFCO had also destroyed at least one of those railroads upon leaving its area of operation.

In 1954, the democratically elected Guatemalan government of Colonel Jacobo Arbenz Guzmán was toppled by U.S.-backed forces led by Colonel Carlos Castillo Armas who invaded from Honduras. Assigned by the Eisenhower administration, this military opposition was armed, trained and organized by the U.S. Central Intelligence Agency.

The directors of United Fruit Company (UFCO) had lobbied to convince the Truman and Eisenhower administrations that Colonel Arbenz intended to align Guatemala with the Soviet Bloc. Besides the disputed issue of Arbenz's allegiance to Communism, UFCO was being threatened by the Arbenz government's agrarian reform legislation and new Labor Code.

Vested Interests In High Places

United States Secretary of State was John Foster Dulles whose law firm Sullivan and Cromwell had represented United Fruit. His brother Allen Dulles was the director of the CIA, and a board member of United Fruit.

Ed Whitman, who was United Fruit's principal lobbyist, was married to President Eisenhower's personal secretary, Ann C. Whitman. Many individuals who directly influenced U.S. policy towards Guatemala in the 1950s also had direct ties to UFCO.

Company holdings in Cuba, which included sugar mills in the Oriente region of the island, were expropriated by the 1959 revolutionary government led by Fidel Castro. By April 1960 Castro was accusing the company of aiding Cuban exiles and supporters of former leader Fulgencio Batista in initiating a seaborn invasion of Cuba directed from the United States. Castro warned the U.S. that "Cuba is not another Guatemala" in one of many combative diplomatic exchanges before the failed Bay of Pigs invasion of 1961.

PR Pioneers

Finally, United Fruit are notable for pioneering PR. They were clients of Edward Bernays, Freud's nephew and not coincidentally the godfather of public relations. Applying the principles of Freudian psychology to advertising, Bernays developed the ideas of product placement, celebrity endorsement, and selling things with sex.

For United Fruit, he publicized their (occasional) philanthropic endeavours in Central America, made educational films and radio programmes, and set up a Middle America Information Bureau to inform journalists about the realities of life in the growing regions. He encouraged United Fruit to donate to the exploration of the archaeological ruins that had been uncovered in the course of their jungle-clearing.

Bananagate

In 1975, the U.S. Securities and Exchange Commission exposed a scheme by United Brands (dubbed Bananagate) to bribe Honduran President Oswaldo López Arellano with US$1.25 million, plus the promise of another US$1.25 million upon the reduction of certain export taxes. Trading in United Brands stock was halted and López was ousted in a military coup.

Banana Massacre

One of the most notorious strikes by United Fruit workers broke out on 12 November 1928 on the Caribbean coast of Colombia, near Santa Marta.

On December 6, Colombian Army troops allegedly under the command of General Cortés Vargas, opened fire on a crowd of strikers gathered in the central square of the town of Ciénaga. Estimates of the number of casualties vary from 400 to 2000.

The military justified this action by claiming that the strike was subversive and its organizers were Communist revolutionaries. Congressman Jorge Eliécer Gaitán claimed that the army had acted under instructions from the United Fruit Company. The ensuing scandal contributed to President Miguel Abadía Méndez's Conservative Party being voted out of office in 1930, putting an end to 44 years of Conservative rule in Colombia.

The Columbian government claimed that they had to resort to the military action on the innocent strikers as they feared a US invasion.

There may be a grain of truth in this claim as US military was used in Mexico, the Caribbean, and Central America close to 30 times prior to the 1929 massacre for the purposes of putting down strikes and generally making large areas of land in other countries "safe for bananas". Howard Zinn wrote quite a bit about US military interventions on behalf of United Fruit in his People's History of the United States.

The telegram from Bogotá Embassy to the U.S. Secretary of State, dated December 5, 1928, stated:

"I have been following Santa Marta fruit strike through United Fruit Company representative here; also through Minister of Foreign Affairs who on Saturday told me government would send additional troops and would arrest all strike leaders and transport them to prison at Cartagena; that government would give adequate protection to American interests involved."

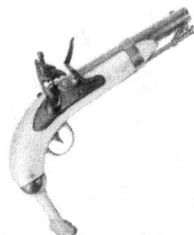

The telegram from Bogotá Embassy to Secretary of State, date December 7, 1928, stated:

"Situation outside Santa Marta City unquestionably very serious: outside zone is in revolt; military who have orders "not to spare ammunition" have already killed and wounded about fifty strikers. Government now talks of general offensive against strikers as soon as all troopships now on the way arrive early next week."

The Dispatch from US Bogotá Embassy to the US Secretary of State, dated December 29, 1928, stated:

"I have the honor to report that the legal advisor of the United Fruit Company here in Bogotá stated yesterday that the total number of strikers killed by the Colombian military authorities during the recent disturbance reached between five and six hundred; while the number of soldiers killed was one."

The Dispatch from US Bogotá Embassy to the US Secretary of State, dated January 16, 1929, stated:

"I have the honor to report that the Bogotá representative of the United Fruit Company told me yesterday that the total number of strikers killed by the Colombian military exceeded one thousand."

The surviving strikers of the massacre were immediately put in jail and executed. There were many other small strikes that were inspired by the one that caused the banana massacre.

The Banana massacre is said to be one of the main events that preceded the Bogotazo, the subsequent era of violence known as La Violencia, and the guerrillas who developed during the bipartisan National Front period, creating the ongoing armed conflict in Colombia.

The more self-reliant people become in third world countries, the less they need the products of the global economy. If they replace the export crops that have been foisted on them and grow locally adapted food crops, they won't need to import American grain. In the history of the world, every place where humans have prospered has provided them with the food and fiber and building materials that they needed, for if food wouldn't grow (like in Antarctica and the Sahara), people didn't stick around long.

People are naturally self-reliant and it takes quite a social derangement to keep them from building adequate shelters and growing adequate food. Corporate imperialists are exporters of social derangement. They build a pipeline to the resources of an area and hook it up to a vacuum, pulling out things of value and leaving only pollution behind. The sooner that indigenous peoples take up arms against the visiting corporatist who is casing the joint, the better off they will be.

~ Daniel Rodriguez

That day marked a turning point, the end of a hopeful age of reform and the beginning of a bloody age of revolution and reaction. Over the next four decades, hundreds of thousands of people — 200,000 in Guatemala alone — were killed in guerrilla attacks, government crackdowns and civil wars across Latin America.

A resident of Bogota provides an epitaph: "Look at the mess we've got ourselves into just because we invited a gringo to eat some bananas."

Reference

Lamb, H. 2009, Fighting the banana wars and other Fairtrade battles: how we took on the corporate giants to change the world, Rider, London.

Bucheli, Marcelo (2005). Bananas and Business: The United Fruit Company in Colombia: 1899–2000. New York: New York University Press.

Schoultz, Lars (1998). Beneath the United States. Harvard University Press.

Stanley, Diane K. (1994). For the Record: The United Fruit Company's Sixty-six Years in Guatemala. Guatemala City: Editorial Antigua.

When civilization is disconnected from the loving relation of the Supreme Personality of Godhead, symptoms like changes of seasonal regulations, foul means of livelihood, greed, anger and fraudulence become rampant. The change of seasonal regulations refers to one season's atmosphere becoming manifest in another season -- for example the rainy season's being transferred to autumn, or the fructification of fruits and flowers from one season in another season. A godless man is invariably greedy, angry and fraudulent.

~ Srila Prabhupada (Srimad Bhagavatam 1.14.3)

19

The GM Genocide In India

Thousands of indian farmers are committing suicide after using genetically modified crops.

When Prince Charles claimed thousands of Indian farmers were killing themselves after using GM crops, he was branded a scaremonger. In fact, situation is even worse than he feared. Beguiled by the promise of future riches, thousands of farmers are borrowing money in order to buy the GM seeds. But when the harvests fail, they are left with spiralling debts - and no income.

Thousands of farmers have taken their own life as a result of the ruthless drive to use India as a testing ground for genetically modified crops. The crisis, branded the 'GM Genocide' by campaigners, was highlighted when Prince Charles claimed that the issue of GM had become a 'global moral question' - and the time had come to end its unstoppable march.

The price difference is staggering: £10 for 100 grams of GM seed, compared with less than £10 for 1,000 times more traditional seeds.

But GM salesmen and government officials had promised farmers that these were 'magic seeds' - with better crops that would be free from parasites and insects. Indeed, in a bid to promote the uptake of GM seeds, traditional varieties were banned from many government seed banks.

India's economic boom means cities such as Mumbai and Delhi have flourished, while the farmers' lives have slid back into the dark ages. When crops failed in the past, farmers could still save seeds and replant them the following year.

But with GM seeds they cannot do this. GM seeds contain 'terminator technology', so that the resulting crops do not produce viable seeds of their own.

As a result, farmers have to buy new seeds each year at the same punitive prices. For some, that means the difference between life and death. Thus the cost of the genetically modified future is murderously high.

Official figures from the Indian Ministry of Agriculture do indeed confirm that it is a huge humanitarian crisis, more than 1,000 farmers are killing themselves each month. According to the National Crime Records Bureau (NCRB), between 1995 and 2009, more than a quarter-million farmers committed suicide.

In 2009 alone, more than 17,000 farmers committed suicide just in the state of Uttar Pradesh.

Some experts believe the actual number of farmer suicides is much higher than official data indicates.

"The official statistics in India rely on the National Crime Records Bureau -- basically what are police reports of suicide," says Professor Prabhat Jha of the Center for Global Health Research in Toronto, according to BBC.

"Suicide is a taboo subject," he adds, suggesting that some deaths have likely been attributed by their families to other causes, like serious illness.

Indian agriculture is in such dire straits that everyday 2000 farmers are quitting agriculture to join the swelling ranks of coolies in urban slums. This fact was reported by International Business Times in a report dated May 02, 2013.

Reference

Andrew Malone, The Daily Mail, 3 November 2008

Bt Cotton and Farmer Suicides in India: Reviewing the Evidence Gruere et al, IFPRI (2008)

Srijit Mishra, Suicide of Farmers in Maharashtra IGIDR, Mumbai (January 2006)

National Crime Reports Bureau, ADSI Report Annual – 2012 Government of India.

Nitin Sethi, 14,000 farmers ended life in 2011 The Times of India (July 2, 2012)

20

India

An Illusion of Independence

Arun Kumar, The Hindu, June 22, 2012

There are enough reasons to suspect that companies overseas influence Indian politics.

Pranab Mukherjee is likely to be India's next President. It seemed to be touch and go until the tide turned in his favour. It has been suggested that the corporates swung it for him not because he is one of the most seasoned Indian politicians but because they wanted him out of the Ministry of Finance. He has acted tough on retrospective taxation and GAAR – the measures in his recent budget to tackle black income generation. But it would not be surprising if the real pressure was from foreign shores. Indian corporates are sensitive to what their foreign counterparts think. So is our political leadership. Britain and Netherlands exerted strong influence on the Vodafone case. How much of our politics is being determined by such pressures?

Pressure On Polity

Several recent events testify that pressure is certainly being exerted on the polity: Hillary Clinton's visit to India to influence the government's policies on trade with Iran and on FDI in retail, the S&P downgrade of India and the Aircel Maxis deal. There are also less visible cases of foreign pressure as in defence purchases (the British were upset at our rejection of the Eurofighter), energy sector investments (oil, gas and nuclear), opening of markets and so on. The Bofors scam has had a continuing impact on politics since 1987. Sten Lindstrom, the former head of the Swedish police who led the investigations into the Bofors-India howitzer deal, recently underlined that there was conclusive evidence that Ottavio Quattarocchi, a close friend of the Nehru-Gandhi family, was one of the recipients of kickbacks. His role in swinging the Bofors deal at the last minute was known. It is not in doubt that payoffs were made or that the Bofors guns are good. The only unsettled issue is who got the money.

That Mr. Quattrochi had powerful friends was confirmed when he was allowed to escape the country. The case was apparently deliberately spoilt by the investigative agencies, including the CBI and, therefore, lost in the courts — in Malaysia, Britain and Argentina. The red corner notice against him "could not be executed" since our police agencies could not "find" him even though journalists could interview him.

Evidence points to a high level cover up. M.S. Solanki, then the External Affairs Minister, sacrificed his Cabinet berth rather than reveal what he wrote in the paper he passed on to the Swiss counterpart at a meeting. At that point of time, the Swiss bank accounts were being investigated by the Indian agencies to trace the Bofors payoff trail. Could such a sacrifice of a political career be for an ordinary leader?

Culture Of Kickbacks

Kickbacks are common globally. Sweden is one of the least corrupt countries in the world but its corporations have bribed to get contracts as the Bofors case shows. U.S.-based multinational corporations have resorted to bribes in spite of their being illegal under that country's law.

Recently, Walmart admitted to having bribed its way through in Mexico. When the top management learnt of it, rather than exposing corruption, the internal probe was closed. The same Walmart has been trying to enter India. Ms Clinton's agenda included "persuading" India to open its doors to foreign retail.

The only Chief Minister she visited was Mamata Banerjee, the important UPA partner opposing FDI in retail. It is reminiscent of Henry Kissinger and the Secretaries of Energy and Defence flying to India to lobby for Enron in the mid-1990s. Enron admitted to spending $60 million in India, to "educate" policymakers.

It is not just a few MNCs that indulge in corruption or use their governments to apply pressure on policies. MNC banks are known to help Indians take their capital out of India. UBS bank, the largest Swiss bank, was fined $750 million by the U.S. for helping its citizens to keep secret bank accounts. The same UBS bank was allowed entry into India in spite of its known role; was it a reward for helping some powerful people?

Executives of Siemens, a supposedly honest MNC and an important player in India, were indicted in the U.S. in December 2011 for bribery in Argentina. Investigations revealed that the company also made illegal payments to the tune of $1.4 billion from 2001 to 2007 in Bangladesh, China, Russia, Venezuela and other countries. These were often routed via 'consultants'. The company paid fines and fees of $1.6 billion to the U.S. and German governments for the bribes it paid across the globe.

Siemens started bribing soon after the end of World War II to get contracts under the Marshall Plan which were mostly going to the Americans. Since its prosecution, Siemens claims to have appointed

A man becomes too greedy for wealth and power when he has no higher objective in life and when he thinks that this earthly life of a few years is all in all. Ignorance is the cause for all these anomalies in human society, and to remove this ignorance, especially in this age of degradation, the powerful sun is there to distribute light in the shape of Srimad-Bhagavatam.

~ Srila Prabhupada (Srimad Bhagavatam 1.14.3)

Compliance Officers to check bribery. But, with the prevalence of a high degree of illegality internationally, can one company be honest while others are not? How would it win contracts when those in charge expect to be bribed? Since non-transparent processes are set up, at every step, decisions need to be influenced, as seen in the Bofors case or the 2G spectrum allocation.

The Vodafone case is significant. MNCs (Indian and foreign) have used tax havens and tax planning to avoid paying taxes in India. They create a web of holdings to hide the identity of the real owners of a company or who it is being transferred to.

In 1985, in the Mcdowell case, the Supreme Court bench observed, "Colourable devices cannot be part of tax planning and it is wrong to encourage or entertain the belief that it is honourable to avoid the payment of tax by resorting to dubious methods".

This judgment was overturned in 2003 in Union of India vs Azadi Bachao Andolan on the use of the Mauritius route to avoid paying tax in India. Vodafone took advantage of this judgment to successfully argue against having to pay capital gains tax in India on transfer of a company in a tax haven which owned the Indian assets. Mr. Mukherjee was trying to recover lost ground.

Dominant Interests

Indian policies have been subject to foreign pressures since the days of the Cold War in the 1950s. But until the mid-1980s, the decisions were accepted as being in the "long-term national interest." There were accusations in the procurement of the Jaguar aircraft also but these did not create the furore that the Bofors scam did. Since the late 1980s, as in the case of Bofors or the new economic policies in 1991 or the Indo-U.S. nuclear deal, sectional or individual interests have become dominant. These have played havoc with national politics. Pressures and counter pressures are mounted through political parties and their leaders and big business.

The lesson is that foreign pressures tend to damage processes that national politics cannot undo. The public is left bewildered by the goings on, as in the present case of selection of the presidential candidate.

(The writer is Chairperson, Centre for Economic Studies and Planning, School of Social Sciences, Jawaharlal Nehru University.)

21

India's Tryst

With Multinational Corporations

The existence of Multinational Corporations (MNCs) in India is approximately three centuries old. As such, the historical background of MNCs in India can be traced back to as early as 1600s whereby the British capital came to dominate the Indian scene through their Multinational Corporation known as East India Company. However, demarcation of the clear boundary lines of this history is hampered by the lack of abundant and authentic data. Moreover, such outlining is also obstructed by the discontinuity in the nature of the data relating to these MNCs. Furthermore, the data available with regard to such FDI in one secondary source do not match with that of another source (Nayak, 2006).

As a result of this, researchers could not portray the complete history of Multinational Corporations and FDI pouring in India even during the post independence era.

To discuss the historical background and policy framework for the MNCs, the analsysis has been divided into two periods i.e. pre and post independence era.

Pre Independence Era Policy

According to Nayak (2006), the period from 1900s-1918 can be called as the first phase of FDI in India when there were no restrictions on the nature as well as type of FDI pouring into India. Majority of these investments at those times were exploitative in nature and were just concentrating in the sectors such as mining and extractive industries to suit the general British economic interest.

It is a noticeable fact that even in the post independence era, a major pie of the FDI source of India continued to come from the same source. It is interesting to note that despite of allowance of this free flow of FDI, no other country was interested in investing in India other than UK and all FDI coming to India during that period were sourced through the Managing Agents from UK

However, the period from 1919-1947 is considered to be more important when the FDI actually originated in India. This phase can be called as second phase of pre-independence FDI history in India. Import duties were introduced during this period to stimulate various British companies to invest in the manufacturing sector in order to protect their businesses in India. Though some Japanese companies also enhanced their trade share with India, yet UK maintained its position as most dominant investor in India during this period.

Post Independence Era Policy

After independence, various issues relating to foreign capital and its accompanying expertise sought attention of the policy makers. With the changing times, the policy of Indian governments kept on changing as per economic and political exigencies prevailing at the time. Accordingly, it can be spilt into four phases (Kumar, 1998 and Chopra, 2003). Whereas in 1960s, these policies were quite liberal, yet these became very stringent in 1970s. However, these were again liberalized in 1980s and real liberalization occurred in 1990s.

But inspite of these changes and modifications in the policies, the underlying principal remained the same - exploitation and plunder. The colonial plunder went on for two centuries but it was not limited to that. They plundered the internal resources of the populace as well by the process of 'mind colonization'.

The slavery was not only physical and financial but intellectual as well. So much so that after India gained independence, post-independence leaders, coloured by the ideas and institutions of Western colonialism largely ignored what were seen as the idiosyncratic views of Mahatma Gandhi, the revered father figure of the Indian independence movement. They preferred the familiar structures of the British Raj. The sad result was the continuation of colonial legacy, at times in its more hideous form. The brown British were to prove worse than the original white British.

And this brings us to the biggest loot ever in mankind's history, the looting of India by her leaders in the post independence era. Trillions of dollars were siphoned off and deposited in the safe heavens of Swiss banking systems while millions died of malnutrition and hunger back home.

Swiss Banking Association report. 2008, gives a break up of countrywise deposits. Here are the top 5 countries.

India—- $1,456 billion
Russia —$ 470 billion
UK ——-$390 billion
Ukraine – $100 billion
China ——$ 96 billion

Source: Swiss Banking Association report 2008

"In an era rife with globalization, transparent business practices and zero tolerance to fraud and misconduct are key concerns for companies doing business in India," according to a recent KPMG India fraud survey report. The global professional services firm found that top-level executives in India were reluctant to discuss the topics of bribery and corruption. Some 71% of survey respondents felt fraud was an inevitable cost of doing business. A global survey by Ernst & Young is equally blunt about the country: "Seventy percent of India respondents to our survey think that bribery and corruption are widespread in the country."

This is more money than all the money in all the banks in India taken together. There is more Indian money in Swiss banks than rest of the world combined.

Is India a poor country? An amount 13 times larger than the country's foreign debt stashed away in secret Swiss accounts, one needs to rethink if India is a poor country. This ill-begotten wealth is even higher than India's GDP and three times that of market capitalisation on national stock exchange.

Corrupt industrialists, politicians, bureaucrats, cricketers, film actors, sex trade and protected wildlife operators, to name just a few, are the accomplices in this historical heist. But this is just the story of Swiss bank accounts. What about other international banks?

By allowing the proliferation of tax havens in the twentieth century, the Western world explicitly encourages the movement of scarce capital from the developing countries.

Often corporations target new markets in developing countries as Nestle did in the 80's and more recently, the tobacco industry. In these and many other cases, corporations deny any health risks to their products, even in the face of overwhelming scientific evidence, in order to maximize profit. Nestlé's fierce marketing of powdered milk in the 80's caused the deaths of an estimated 1.5 million children through the contaminated water used to make the infant formula.

Nor are human rights observed. Chevron and Coca Cola have been indirectly involved in the violent killings of workers and union officials in developing countries in attempts to suppress workers rights. Instances of kidnappings, torture, discrimination, health violations, fuelling conflicts, privatizing and contaminating local water sources, using child labour and even sex trafficking have all been documented as occurring under the responsibility of the largest corporations. Sweatshops are often used in developing countries by the apparel industry which usually pay negligible wages to under age workers who often work long hours in terrible conditions.
~Rajesh Makwana

Reference

Policy framework for multinational, corporations in India-a historical perspective. Dusanjh, Harpreet Sidhu, 09/01/2010, Indian Journal of Economics and Business Publisher.

Rungta, Radhe Shyam. The Rise of the Business Corporation in India, 1851–1900, (1970)

Majumdar, Ramesh Chandra. Corporate Life in Ancient India, (1920)

22

MNCs

Bigger Than Their Assets

The reach and influence of multinationals, large and small, is far greater than the official statistics suggest. Policymakers can, therefore, seriously underestimate the extent to which national economies have become intertwined with others. There are at least two sources for this misconception: the way in which cross-border investments are estimated and the manner in which the "boundary" of a firm is defined.

The official figures for the flow of FDI - the historical cost-accounting basis for the asset base of multinational corporations - show an annual flow of nearly $400 billion. The United Nations, however, has recently begun to question these figures and has estimated that if one includes the capital mobilized by local borrowings and the equity shares of partners, the "real" figure is

From a mere three thousand in 1990 the number of multinationals has grown to over 63,000 today. Along with their 821,000 subsidiaries spread all over the world, these multinational corporations directly employ 90 million people (of whom some 20 million in the developing countries) and produce 25 per cent of the world's gross product. The top 1,000 of these multinationals account for 80 percent of the world's industrial output. With its $210 billion in revenues, ExxonMobil is ranked number 21 among the world's 100 largest economies, just behind Sweden and above Turkey.

closer to $1.4 trillion per year. In other words, a corporation's "presence" in a country goes beyond the assets that it chooses to locate there.

The influence of a multinational can also be gauged by its effect on local suppliers as it creates new demand and sets new standards of quality. All these elements are part of a world where the local production of MNCs in overseas markets now greatly exceeds the sum of world trade. The resulting deep integration of national economies is growing so fast that any suggestion in developed economies that the domestic-policy agenda can be isolated from the global economy seems antediluvian.

Perhaps even more seriously, the explosion of strategic alliances among firms is transforming the competitive landscape. One estimate is that more than 20,000 alliances have been formed within the last two years alone. How, then, should one now think about where economic power is located? As one executive observed some years ago: "The electronics business in Europe is not the same as the European electronics business." Competition is no longer defined solely by the ownership of assets; it is also a matter of who is in league with whom.

Reference

John Stopford, Multinational corporations. Foreign Policy, Winter 1998

Empire (Negri and Hardt book) (2000)

The global economy is in a very precarious state, relying on volatile financial markets and driven increasingly by commercial pressures. Many economists and analysts are predicting a global economic failure sparked by a stock market or financial collapse. This possibility is strengthened by the current conflicts over resources, political instability in many parts of world and the declining strength and influence of the US dollar.

23

In The World's Richest Nation

Nearly Half Of All Households Lack Basic Economic Security: Study

There are certain basic costs that every household runs up -- food costs, medical expenses, utility bills. And almost half of all Americans are in danger of not being able to afford these things.

A recent study from the nonprofit Wider Opportunities for Women (WOW) finds that 45 percent of all Americans -- men, women and children -- live in households that lack economic security, defined as the ability to pay for basic needs like food, transportation and medical care, while setting aside a modest amount of money for emergency and retirement savings.

The WOW report is only the latest indication that for a vast number of people in the U.S., the poor health of the economy is not a distant or abstract concern, but a problem that affects day-to-day decisions about how money can be spent.

Thirty-nine percent of all adults in the country, and 55 percent of all children, live in households that lack economic security, the report finds.

The problem is worse for women than for men -- 74 percent of single mothers are economically insecure, compared with just 49 percent of single fathers -- and worse for people of color than for whites, with just 20 percent of white two-worker households below the economic security line, versus 29 percent for blacks and 43 percent for Hispanics.

These discrepancies across racial and gender lines are likely related to various wage gaps that put white people, especially white men, at an earnings advantage. In 2010, black men earned only 74.5 percent of a typical white man's wage, and women earned 78 cents for every dollar earned by men.

The unemployment crisis is also hitting men and women differently, with the vast majority of jobs created in the past two years going to male workers. In terms of race, the unemployment rate for blacks nationwide is twice that of whites, and the Hispanic rate is almost half again as high as that of whites.

Workers nationwide are also suffering from stagnant wages that, for fully half of the country's workforce, clock in at less than $27,000. People's ability to afford food was recently found to be near a three-year low, and their ability to cover the basic costs of living is currently worse than at any time since the start of 2008.

"Several times my typewriter and tape recorders were stolen and the police could not take any action. There are many persons in the Bowery Street; they have no shelter to live. So if a certain fraction of the people are supposed to be very materially happy at the cost of others, that is not material advancement. Had it been so, then why there are so many persons confused and frustrated? So actually there is no material advancement here. So the Western type of civilization, industrialism and capitalism, is no material advancement. It is material exploitation."
— *Srila Prabhupada (Letter, 14 March 1969)*

All of this is taking place against a backdrop of rising economic inequality, as the country's highest earners continue to draw bigger and bigger paychecks and wealth becomes ever more concentrated among the wealthy.

Source

Alexander Eichler, The Huffington Post, 22/11/2011

Shawn McMahon

Jessica Horning, Living Below the Line: Economic Insecurity and America's Families, Fall 2013

24

In UK, The Former Global Power

Seven Million Working Adults Are 'Just One Bill Away From Disaster'

Nearly seven million working adults are under such financial strain each month a single unforeseen bill could cause them financial disaster, a study has found.

Around 3.6million households were struggling to find enough money at the end of each month to provide food for themselves and their children, according to shocking new research.

The survey for the Guardian focused on people who are employed and not reliant on state welfare, for whom 'work no longer pays'.

It found a squeeze on salaries and spiraling living costs were having a particularly devastating consequences, forcing millions towards poverty.

Some of those facing the most critical financial stress can include a couple, without children, with a gross annual household income of between £12,000 and £29,000, or couples with two children on between £17,000 and £41,000.

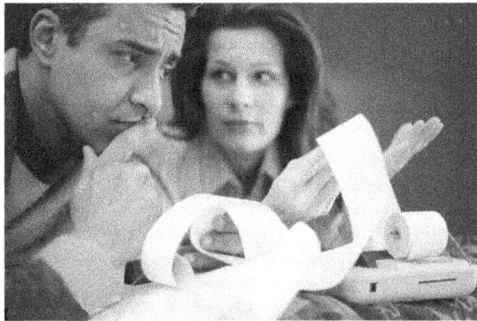

The dire predicament meant they were so stretched that a larger than expected bill could force them into debt, with no equity in their home or savings on which to fall back.

Bruno Rost, head of Experian Public Sector, which conducted the study, told the Guardian: 'These people are the new working class – except the work they do no longer pays.

'These people say that being forced to claim benefits or move into a council property would be the worst kind of social ignominy and self-failure.'

This latest research comes a week after charity Oxfam claimed that of those classed as being in poverty – officially defined as households with income of less than 60 per cent of median average - the number of people working outnumbered those unemployed.

Oxfam's report also found that those in work but claiming housing benefit had risen to 900,000 – more than doubling since 2005.

The growing number of adults being placed under severe financial strain despite being in work and not relying on the state is likely to embarrass the Government which declared that getting a job was the best way to pull families out of poverty.

Iain Duncan Smith recently unveiled plans to remove incentives to stay on welfare rather than moving into work.

Work and Pensions Secretary insisted that employment, not a few extra pounds in welfare benefits, was the key to lifting families

---

The money is to be kept in cattle and grains. That is Indian economy, cattle and grains. If you have got many cows, you get milk. Milk preparation. And if you have got grain, then where is your problem? You prepare your foodstuff at home and eat and chant Hare Krsna. Where is your problem? You want to eat and live peacefully. So if you have got grains and milk, you have got enough food and there is no problem. You haven't got to go fifty miles for your work, and then you require a tin car. So many problems. But if you get your food at home, then eat them and chant Hare Krsna and go back to home, back to Godhead. Simple thing.

(Morning Walk, December 31, 1973, Los Angeles)

out of poverty, as he unveils plans to replace all other out of work benefits from 2013, with the Coalition's new universal credit.

Source
Amelia Hill, The Guardian, 18 June 2012
Tom Gardner, The Daily Mail, 19 June 2012

25

Globalisation Of Corruption

Further Case Studies

Today, often on a daily basis, television and newspaper headlines are filled with corporate corruption scandals that range, from minor cases of individual corruption to multi-billion dollar corporate collapses that shock the conscience of society.

Corruption is a corrosive drain on public trust and on the legitimacy of public and private sector institutions. Its toll can be devastating to a national economy, particularly at a time when open global markets can rapidly reverse investment and capital flows if confidence and trust are compromised by revelations of systemic corruption.

According to a report Sue Hawley and published by the NGO, The Corner House, the growth of corruption across the globe is largely the result of rapid privatization of public enterprises, along with 'reforms' to downsize and undervalue civil services, pushed on developing countries by the World Bank, the IMF and western governments supporting their transnational corporations.

The report estimates that western businesses pay bribes to the tune of $80 billion a year - roughly the amount that the United Nations believes is needed to eradicate global poverty.

"There is seldom just one cockroach in the kitchen"
~Warren Buffet (Stanford Business Magazine, August 2008)

SGS And Hubco, Pakistan

In April 1999, Benazir Bhutto and her husband were found guilty of accepting bribes worth US$ 9m from SGS, were sentenced to five years in prison, and banned from holding seats in parliament for seven years (the defendants appealed against this judgement) (Australian Business Intelligence, 26 April 1999). However, the multinational escaped with no punishment. A group in Pakistan had to apply to the Lahore High Court complaining that SGS 'was still operating in the country despite the fact that the court had convicted one party as being the guilty of the corruption'; and obtained a ruling barring the government from 'allocating any business to SGS' (Business Recorder, 17 May 1999 and 30 May 1999).

Hubco Case

The government of Pakistan has been pursuing cases of alleged bribery of members of the previous regime, especially in energy. Two contracts - one involving Southern Company (USA) (reported in the South China Morning Post, 7 July 1997), and one involving National Grid (UK) (Financial Times, 24 April 1997) were cancelled on the grounds that they had been improperly obtained. The government also took proceedings against existing contracts, investigating alleged corruption, and stating that it would cut the price of electricity agreed under these contracts. The main target of these investigations was Hubco, the largest stock exchange quoted company in Pakistan, which is 26 per cent owned by National Power, a UK energy multinational.

Under the spell of ignorance, one cannot understand a thing as it is. For example, everyone can see that his grandfather has died and therefore he will also die; man is mortal. The children that he conceives will also die. So death is sure. Still, people are madly accumulating money and working very hard all day and night, not caring for the eternal spirit. This is madness. In their madness, they are very reluctant to make advancement in spiritual understanding.

~ Srila Prabhupada (Bhagavad Gita 14.8)

World Bank: No Loan Unless Contracts Left Alone

When the Pakistan government insisted that power tariffs should be reduced because of the evidence that corruption had led to inflated prices, this 'drew anxious reactions' from many, including the World Bank. Senior government officials say the Bank has urged Pakistan to keep its so-called investigations into alleged corruption in Hubco's contract separate from the future of the company's tariff. The future of an International Monetary Fund agreement, currently under negotiation in Islamabad, is also partly tied to the extent to which Pakistan resolves its dispute with the power companies' (Financial Times, 18 November 1998).

At the end of 1998, the Bank authorised the IMF to proceed with a US$1.3 billion bailout package for Pakistan, 'as it was satisfied with the government assurances for out of court settlement of two-year long row with the Independent Power Producers' (The Nation, 31 December 1998).

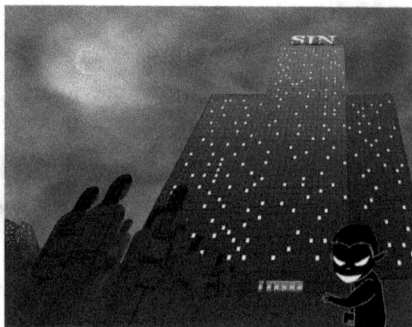

At no stage did the UK government appear to have supported the Pakistan government's decision to prosecute Hubco for corruption. The company's chief executive is now living in the 'safe haven' of Cheshire, having 'fled Pakistan following threats that he might be arrested' (Financial Times, 27 October 1998).

The British and other governments actively supported the World Bank's position that Pakistan had to resolve Hubco impasse before it can expect any financial help. (The Nation, 30 December 1998). In

Indian officials have raided the offices of Vodafone India, a subsidiary of Vodafone Plc of the U.K., in connection with the massive irregularities in 2G spectrum allocation and following close on the heels of a renewed US$2.54 billion tax demand on the company.

February 1999, a UK government minister emphasised that the action against Hubco was a step backwards for 'investor confidence', rather than a step forward in the fight against corruption:

'Minister of State for Foreign and Commonwealth Affairs Derek Fatchett told a news conference in Karachi that the longer the row continued the more it would damage Pakistan's prospects for attracting foreign investment. "Let me say this is an issue in my opinion that has gone on for much too long. It is an issue that needs to be resolved. It is an issue that is damaging investor confidence in Pakistan," he said at the end of a three-day trip' (Reuters, 10 February 1999).

French-Canadian Consortium, Mexico

The 1997 local elections in Mexico City resulted in a landslide victory for the opposition, which had campaigned on an anti-corruption platform. The party promised to review all contracts awarded by the outgoing administration, and cancel those in which irregularities were detected.

One casualty was a US$400m contract for rolling stock for the Mexico City metro, which had been awarded to a French-Canadian consortium. The response of the French and Canadian governments, at the highest possible level, showed little interest in the question of corruption:

President Jacques Chirac of France and Jean Chretien, the Canadian prime minister, have sent strongly worded letters to Ernesto Zedillo, the Mexican president, protesting at the way a French-Canadian consortium was disqualified from a US$400m tender to provide rolling stock for the Mexico City metro. A new tender for the metro rolling

One of the most scandalous cases was in the 1980s where the US chemical business Union Carbide tolerated very poor safety standards at a factory in Bhopal, India. The result was an explosion which released clouds of toxic gas and killed thousands. Many more thousands are still alive and very ill because of this. What was particularly irresponsible was the long years it took to force Union Carbide to accept responsibility and pay compensation.

stock is expected only after Cuauhtémoc Cardenas, the mayor-elect, takes office in December and appoints a new management for the Mexico City metro. In his letter to President Zedillo, Mr Chretien lamented Mexico's inadequate legal safeguards for foreign investors'. (Financial Times, 3 October 1997)

EDS In Czech Republic

In the Czech Republic in 1998, in the case of a US computer firm EDS, the US embassy responded to public accusations of corruption not with encouragement to investigate but with a bland statement:

The US embassy told CTK today that it had no information to suggest that the US computer firm EDS had bribed the former Christian Democrat (KDU-CSL) government in order to win lucrative defence contracts for the new army command information system. The embassy also said that it could not confirm claims that EDS had been warned on at least two occasions by embassy officials that it was under suspicion of corruption. (Czech News Agency, 24 July 1998)

Indeed, the embassy invoked the existence of the FCPA (Foreign Corrupt Practices Act) as evidence that a US company would not be corrupt:

The embassy added that US firms operating abroad were bound by the 1977 Foreign Corrupt Practices Act, which clearly bans offering of bribes in order to win contracts. If an American firm was found guilty of offering bribes in the Czech Republic it would also have to face

The failure of the global economy and the existing aid and development programs to address poverty and inequality is apparent. At the heart of this failure is the competitive, profit driven, self interest of economically dominant nations. Modern, multinational corporations are the embodiments of these traits, and they play a key role in sustaining the status quo through their economic and political influence.

responsibility back home in the US, and would at least lose the right to compete for US government orders, it went on. (ibid.)

AES, Norpak Hydroelectric Schemes, Uganda

There were two proposals to build private hydroelectric power schemes in Uganda - one at Bugali Falls, by a consortium led by US multinational AES - and one at Owen Falls to be built by the Norwegian company Norpak. Corruption allegations arose in respect to both.

Ugandan MPs repeatedly refused to authorise the schemes because they believed them to be against Uganda's interests; but the World Bank's intervention focused on providing financial support and guarantees to AES, while insisting on yet more privatisation.

In April 1999, six MPs were allegedly compromised by accepting a week's trip to Norway, arranged by Norpak. The politicians denied that they had been compromised:

'Six MPs who have just returned from a one-week trip to Norway to inspect Norpak projects yesterday said they have no apologies to offer over the trip. They defended their trip saying, "We were duly

---

Walmart has been in the news in India because it was perceived as one of the principal beneficiaries of the contentious new foreign direct investment (FDI) policy in multi-brand retail. Then the company revealed that its joint venture in India -- Bharti Walmart -- had suspended its chief financial officer and some members of its legal team after an anti-corruption probe.

The scrutiny facing Walmart intensified when newspapers claimed that the company had been lobbying in India to woo Members of Parliament to its side in the FDI vote. The Lok Sabha (the lower house of Parliament) was totally paralyzed for a couple of days and, on January 24, 2013, the government appointed a one-man panel to probe the charges. Walmart says the lobbying was done in Washington, where it is legal, and not in New Delhi, where it is not.

The Walmart inquiry started from a New York Times report about bribery by the retail giant in Mexico. Further investigation uncovered that the corruption charges spread to India, China and Brazil.

nominated by Parliament Speaker, Mr. Francis Ayume, following an invitation by Norpak'" (New Vision, 28 April 1999).

The cost of the trip was reportedly not paid by the company, but by the Norwegian state:

'The bills, that include: first class accommodation, air tickets and shopping in Norway, were reportedly paid by the Norwegian embassy' (New Vision, 21 April 1998).

Undermining The Judicial Authority

The lack of enthusiasm for anti-corruption investigations echoes the readiness of the multinationals and their business associations to undermine the authority of judicial institutions when they rule against the companies' interests.

Early in 1997, for example, trade unionists and environmentalists in the Philippines brought court cases against the proposed water privatisation in Manila. Formal protests by the entire business community of OECD countries were used to insist that the courts should not rule against western business interests. The courts

Corruption like other forms of entrepreneurship has evolved considerably. A few years after liberalization, Enron admitted to a U.S. Congressional committee that it had spent US$20 million to "educate Indians" on the benefits of its power project in Maharashtra. Today, the money moves more subtly. In telecommunications, for instance, Indian companies acquired licenses at a knock-down price from the government with the aid of corrupt ministers. They then sold stakes in the companies that held these licenses to foreign telecom majors seeking an entry into India. The foreign companies paid several times what the Indian entities had shelled out for the licenses. On paper, they look foolish, but not criminal. All the players would have been happy if the Supreme Court hadn't stepped in and cancelled the process. The art of graft has advanced fast.

With new scams and scandals vying for attention, the older ones often fall by the wayside. The politicians shrug off the allegations and are back in positions of power in no time.

~S. Raghunath, Professor Of Corporate Strategy And Policy, Indian Institute Of Management, Bangalore

had already displeased the government with rulings which went against their privatisation policies. The reported reaction of the multinationals and their governments showed little respect for the due process of law:

'Loud complaints about "terrorists in robes" have resonated in government and business circles in the past month as the courts delivered a series of blows to investor confidence with controversial rulings against the state's privatisation programme.' (Bangkok Post, 14 February 1997)

This is part of a general unwillingness by multinationals to accept the authority of courts in developing countries. When the government of Maharashtra in India decided to end or renegotiate an energy deal with Enron, the company sought arbitration in London; when the province of Tucuman in Argentina terminated the water concession that had been awarded to Générale des Eaux, the company referred its dispute to the World Bank for arbitration.

In some cases, governments of OECD countries act as 'official channels' for payments which could be considered corrupt.

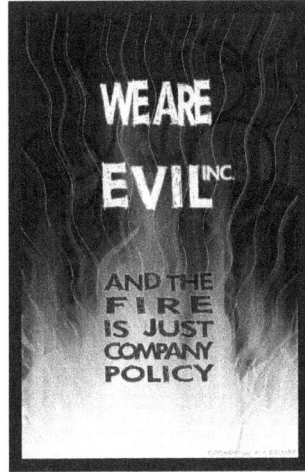

If all else fails, financial accounts can be adjusted to create the impression of profit and growth. This was the case in numerous corporate scandals and the collapse of corporations such as Enron. Its case simultaneously implicated many other sectors of the accounting and banking industry, such as Arthur Andersen and the National Westminster Bank, who were taken in by and facilitated Enron's false accounting, financing and fraudulent activities. Of course the big losers were the 21,000 employees who not only lost their jobs, but their pension plans and savings which were all tied to Enron stock.

~ Rajesh Makwana

Water Privatisation, Indonesia

In 1997, while Jakarta was still under the control of president Suharto, its water supply was privatised, under the auspices of the World Bank. One concession went to a consortium led by Thames Water (UK), another to a consortium led by Lyonnaise des Eaux (France). Both consortia included partners which were owned by friends of the president. After Suharto's fall, even the consortia accepted that these concessions were no longer defensible. The multinationals moved rapidly with new 'clean' companies to negotiate new contracts with Jakarta City Council, to run from February 1999.

But these contracts have been subject to bitter criticism on the grounds that they were never properly advertised, that the prices contained in them are excessive, and that Suharto's son continued to hold five per cent equity in the new Thames Water venture. Court action has been taken to have the contracts declared void, and a trade union of water workers has demanded that the contracts be rescinded (Asia Pulse, 29 April 1999).

The original concession awards under the Suharto regime had been made under the auspices of a World Bank-supported tendering procedure, yet the Bank made no public statement calling for investigation of the alleged corruption. On the contrary, three weeks before the June 1999 general election, it announced new loans of US$400m-US$300m for the water sector.

Reference

de Brie, Christian (2000) 'Thick as thieves' Le Monde Diplomatique (April)

Friedrichs, David O. (2010). Trusted Criminals: White-collar Crime in Contemporary Society.

Gobert, J & Punch, M. (2003). Rethinking Corporate Crime, London: Butterworths.

Znoj, Heinzpeter (2009). "Deep Corruption in Indonesia: Discourses, Practices, Histories".

Morris, S.D. (1991), Corruption and Politics in Contemporary Mexico. University of Alabama Press, Tuscaloosa

Jerry W. Markham, A financial history of modern U.S. corporate scandals: from Enron to reform

26

Manipulating Public Opinion

Public Relations, Marketing and Advertising

The revolutionary shift that we are witnessing at the beginning of the 21st Century from democracy to corporate rule is as significant as the shift from monarchy to democracy, which ushered in the modern age of nation states. It represents a wholesale change in cultural values and aspirations.[1]

This eclipse of democratic values by corporate values is not a natural evolution but the consequence of a deliberate strategy employed by corporate executives who have combined their financial and political resources to spread free market ideology. Corporations, individually and in concert, have utilised all the major communication institutions of a modern society – including the media and education – to shape community beliefs, values and behaviour. This has enabled corporations 'to enthral and becloud the understanding' of large numbers of citizens so that it is commonly believed that large corporations are benevolent institutions that should be minimally regulated because what is good for them is good for society as a whole.[2]

Throughout the 20th Century business associations and coalitions coordinated mass propaganda campaigns that combined sophisticated public relations techniques developed in 20th Century America with revitalised free market ideology originating in 18th

Century Europe. The purpose of this propaganda onslaught has been to persuade a majority of people that it is in their interests to eschew their own power as workers and citizens, and forego their democratic right to restrain and regulate business activity. As a result the political agenda is now largely confined to policies aimed at furthering business interests.[3]

The public relations industry has basically compromised the integrity of the opinion expressed in the public domain by giving the illusion of independence to arguments that are essentially self serving. This is done primarily by a kind of ideological ventriloquism — putting the arguments into the mouths of people/institutions/authorities with important sounding titles that appear to be independent of those forwarding the arguments. PR in this sense is nothing short of an attempt by those that can afford it to buy credibility, integrity, and/or independence for arguments that stem from self interests — essentially an attempt to hide the self serving nature of the arguments.

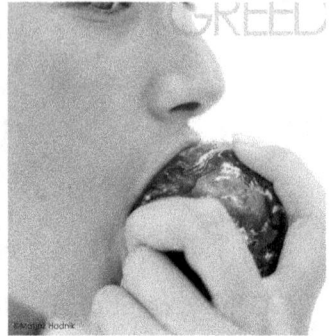

Since the 70's, as public objection to corporate rule and environmental degradation increased, corporations have mounted a successful campaign to increase corporate rights and win back public opinion. This initiative saw the rise of corporate sponsored

All major corporations, particularly those which have the greatest negative impact upon the environment, have repackaged themselves recently as having 'green' credentials to great effect. The oil giant BP's new green, flower-like logo and recent PR campaign is an excellent example. As a result, BP has successfully managed to shift public focus away from the fact that it is one of the world's foremost polluters of the environment and considered by many as one of the top 10 corporate criminals.

law firms who fiercely defended corporate interests by, for example, opposing environmental and social standards and regulations. Such organizations were presented as 'public interest' groups in an attempt to equate public and corporate interests whilst masking corporate involvement. They included environmental and consumer groups that are nothing more than extensions of corporate lobbying in disguise, promoting environmental and commercial deregulation. The academic world was also targeted as corporations funded programs and research in economics and law that favoured neo-liberal ideals. The success of the public relations campaign was guaranteed by their huge financial resources and broad coalition across business groups.[4]

In order to influence policy more directly, conservative policy think tanks were established, such as the Heritage Foundation, the American Enterprise institute and the Cato institute. Influential Business Roundtables made up of CEOs were also established in the 70's, enabling representatives from broad spectrums of industry to actively campaign for the common agenda of economic globalization. Currently almost 200,000 public relations employees in the US actively manipulate public opinion to the advantage of their corporate sponsors.[5]

Far from supplying public demand, corporations actively dictate cultural habits and create demand by influencing the public mind through a sophisticated and well funded combination of research, marketing, advertising and media manipulation. The result is the subtle, but quite apparent, alignment of public and corporate interest. This cultural homogenization of society both nationally and globally is fertile ground for maximizing profit. Whilst levels of unnecessary

At present, the battle for control of the democratic process is being won by the corporate elite. The phenomenon of market forces is becoming more entrenched in every aspect of public life, even influencing our subconscious minds, conscious attitudes and behaviour. As many industrialized nations call for democracy to be spread globally, the economic ideologies they have vested our future in are cancerous to these same democratic principles.

and unsustainable consumption increase globally, corporate longevity is secured. This non consensual capitalization of the public by the wealthy few is another example of an undemocratic process resulting from excessive financial capability and political influence. The sophistication and effectiveness of advertising and marketing methods is well understood. The ubiquity of the television and the increasing number of hours it is watched, especially by children, is particularly disturbing. In the US, watching TV is the 3rd most time consuming pastime, after sleeping and working. In the US, 75% of commercial television time and 50% of public television time is paid for by the 100 largest corporations. Projected global advertising expenditure for corporations in 2006 is over $427 billion dollars.[6]

As traditional markets are saturated, or public opinion turns against a particular product, corporations, using the same aggressive marketing, shift their **COMMUNITY NOT CORPORATION** attention to developing countries with devastating effect. Nestle is notorious for its aggressive marketing of infant formula in poor countries in the 1980s. Because of this practice, Nestle is still one of the most boycotted corporations in the world, and its infant formula is still controversial. In Italy in 2005, police seized more than two million litres of Nestle infant formula that was contaminated with

> *kamasyantam hi ksut-trdbhyam*
> *krodhasyaitat phalodayat*
> *jano yati na lobhasya*
> *jitva bhuktva diso bhuvah*
>
> *The strong bodily desires and needs of a person disturbed by hunger and thirst are certainly satisfied when he eats. Similarly, if one becomes very angry, that anger is satisfied by chastisement and its reaction. But as for greed, even if a greedy person has conquered all the directions of the world or has enjoyed everything in the world, still he will not be satisfied.*
>
> *~ Srila Prabhupada (Srimad Bhagavatam 7.15.20)*

the chemical isopropylthioxanthone (ITX). In recent years, as public awareness of dire health consequences of smoking tobacco have come to light in industrialized nations, tobacco giants have had to shift their focus to increasing demand in developing countries. The WHO has reported that 84% of the estimated 1.3 billion smokers live in developing and transitional economy countries. A 1994 WHO report estimated that the use of tobacco resulted in an annual global net loss of US$ 200 billion, a third of this loss being in developing countries, stumping development efforts.[7]

Education

The education system provides arguably the most fertile ground on which to influence public opinion. In the US, corporations are making significant in-roads by sponsoring teaching materials and aggressively marketing and supplying junk foods through vending machines and lunch programs. Of greatest concern are corporate sponsored curriculum modules, public education propaganda videos, and grants and sponsorship programs that refocus education to pro-corporate aspects of law and economics. Competition, economic growth and profitability are emphasized- qualities that secure future corporate opportunity. There is a simultaneous shift away from learning the benefits of cooperation, community endeavor and goodwill. Together such tactics effectively skew public opinion from an early age and further enshrine the neo-liberal, corporate agenda. Unsurprisingly there is a trend in the US, the EU and developing countries for corporations to operate public schools for profit, capitalizing on yet another market opportunity.[8]

References:
[1][2][3], The Corporate Assault on Democracy, Sharon Beder
[4][5][6][7][8], Rajesh Makwana, October 2006
Manufacturing Consent: Noam Chomsky and the Media
Manufacturing Consent: The Political Economy of the Mass Media (1988),

Corporations

The Centrally Planned Economies

The argument is that centrally planned economies are less efficient and are unresponsive to consumer demand. They argue that to achieve efficiency, government intervention needs to be reduced to a minimum and the democratic, public control of the economy minimized. Thus, free trade and neoliberal policies are being actively promoted through international bodies such as the WTO, World Bank and IMF.

However, this argument is flawed. For a start, corporations are themselves centrally planned economies. Decisions are not open to question within a corporation and absolute control is exercised over production and distribution networks by management. Also, whereas public companies are required to be transparent to public scrutiny, the contracts that corporations have with respect to resource management or service delivery remain a commercial secret, removing an important level of accountability.

Many of these unaccountable corporations now have a greater turnover than the GDP of most countries. Of the 100 largest economies in the world, 52 are corporations and 48 are countries, and these corporations have sales figures between $51 billion and $247 billion.

Corporations

Bringing About Inequality And Unemployment

Seventy percent of world trade is controlled by just 500 of the largest industrial corporations, and in 2002, the top 200 had combined sales equivalent to 28% of world GDP. However, these 200 corporations only employed 0.82% of the global work force, highlighting the reduction in employment created by excessive economies of scale.

In the US, ninety-eight percent of all companies account for only 25 percent of business activity; the remaining two percent account for nearly 75 percent of the remaining activity.

The top 500 industrial corporations, which represent only one-tenth of one percent of all US companies, control over two-thirds of the business resources in the US and collect over 70 percent of all US profits. Thus there is also a disproportionate distribution of financial benefit from economic activity, which clearly does not pass to local communities through opportunity or wages. It is retained instead by a small number of major shareholders of an even smaller number of corporations.

Whereas corporations are based mainly in affluent countries such as the US, the EU, Japan, Canada and Australia, their key markets, productive facilities and many of their resources are based in or extracted from developing countries. According to the International Finance Corporation (IFC), inflows of foreign direct investment to the emerging markets have grown by an average of 23 percent per year between 1990 and 2000. The combined value of stock markets in emerging economies is set to exceed $5 trillion in 2006, and has more than doubled in the past decade.

As corporations grow, they find it economically beneficial (profitable) to operate in multiple countries, seeking out favourable conditions such as low labour costs, fewer regulations and other financial or tax incentives. Many of these multinational corporations can now be described as 'transnational', as they have 'globalized' their operations and retain no particular affiliation to any country. This allows them greater flexibility in operative structure and greater leverage over governments who compete for their business.

The convergence of economic power has created a concentration of political influence in society which is reflected nationally and globally. The resulting influence of the private sector has manipulated global economic, political and public thinking and established an unsustainable, consumerist culture.

As a result of mergers, acquisitions and jobs being transferred abroad (in line with globalized market forces), job losses even in affluent countries are common. Between 1980 and 1993, over four million jobs were shed by the largest 500 industrial corporations

Extensive legislation now exists internationally and within countries to protect corporate rights. Therefore, wide-ranging structural and regulatory changes are essential if we are to transform the corporate led economy into one centered on communities that actively participate in political and economic life. The prioritization of community based enterprise and the curtailing of mega corporate entities will inevitably create greater social equity in both the East and West.

in the US. Since President Bush took office, two million lost their jobs and in 2004 nearly one in ten could not find a full time job.

The International Labor Organization (ILO) calculates that global unemployment rates are at an all time high. Of the 2.8 billion workers in the world in 2005, nearly 1.4 billion still did not earn enough to lift themselves and their families above the two dollars a day poverty line - the same proportion as ten years ago.

Sadly, the prevalence in recent years, of huge corporations has significantly impacted on small businesses and communities, and is creating a homogenization of culture throughout the world. These corporations have created huge economies of scale which result in a downward levelling of job numbers, wages and employment standards. The most visible culprits are agri-business, giant fast food chains and retail outlets such as supermarkets. The goods supplied by these companies have quickly replaced local businesses who often supply the same goods with greater levels of nutrition and with negligible social and environmental consequences.

The effects are visible and measurable in society. For example, in the 10 years that Wal-Mart moved to Iowa, in the USA, 7326 local business closed as a direct result. In the UK, the supermarket giant, Tesco, currently opens one new 'Tesco Express' (a smaller, local version of their larger stores) each day. This results in a local grocer going out of business each day, and 50 local specialist stores close each week. The impact on the developing world is also stark as corporations move steadily into emerging markets. India has recently experienced a surge in contracts to large agri-business firms as the government pursues the high output agricultural policies of the US and EU. This has resulted in entire villages being put up for sale in some states and, according to the National Sample Survey Organization (NSSO), more than 40 per cent of Indian farmers are keen to quit agriculture altogether as a result of these market pressures. In addition, the competitive activity of multinationals has helped to sustain an unfair international trading regime that increases global inequality through biased trade rules and increases global warming through inefficient import and export networks.

It is imperative that these trends are reversed, and that community involvement in economic life is strengthened and safeguarded.

The substantial benefits gained from streamlining operations serve mainly to increase profits, and are channelled into bonuses for directors and CEOs. Chevron's CEO received $37 million in total compensation in 2005, whilst Exxon's CEO received a $400 million pay and retirement package. In the meanwhile the minimum wage in a country like America (£5.15 per hour) is at a 50 year low.

Whilst global economic growth remains slow, at around three percent, corporate growth is around four times as high, again reflecting the concentration of financial gain from a global economy led by corporations. In the year 2005, the number of millionaires globally swelled to a phenomenal 8.7 million, 5.7 million of whom are based in North America and Europe. In addition, Forbes reported a 15% rise in the number of billionaires since last year alone, virtually all have made their fortune from their involvement in various sectors of industry and are now worth a combined $2.6 trillion.

(Source: Rajesh Makwana, October 2006)

> "There is a spiritual hunger in the world today - and it cannot be satisfied by better cars on longer credit terms" - Adlai E. Stevenson

29

AIG CEO Robert Benmosche

80-Year-Old Europeans Need To Be Working

People Are Already Working Longer Than Ever Before In History

This isn't your grandpa's economy. But it could still be yours once you're his age.

Robert Benmosche, chief executive of the recently bailed-out and largely government-owned American International Group, told Bloomberg from his seaside villa that he thinks the eurozone debt crisis will push the retirement age in the region way up.

"Retirement ages will have to move to 75, 80 years old," he said. "That would make pensions, medical services more affordable. They will keep people working longer and will take that burden off of the youth."

In April 2012, world leaders called an emergency meeting to discuss the crisis, as a Spanish banking meltdown and looming Greek election threatened to break up the Eurozone.

One major source of debt for many of the countries in panic mode is generous pensions. One way out: Getting employees to have longer careers, according to Benmosche.

For his part, the 68-year-old AIG chief told the company's shareholders late last year that he planned to stay on longer than he originally anticipated.

Though Benmosche's comments were directed at Europe, American workers may also be working well into their golden years. Already one quarter of middle-class Americans expect to retire when they're 80, not 65, according to a Wells Fargo survey from November.

In addition, the average retirement age of American workers hit 67, according to a Gallup poll from last month. That's up from 63 ten years ago and 60 in the mid-1990s.

Fed Up Man Cuts Off Foot To Continue Claiming Jobless Benefits – Only To Discover He Is Still Eligible For Work

An unemployed man almost died after cutting his own foot off so he could stay on jobless benefits has been told he might still qualify for work despite his amputation.

Hans Url, 56, had just been told his hand-outs would stop if he did not accept work found for him by job centre staff.

And when his claims that he was too sick and did not like the work were challenged with the offer of a medical, he took drastic measures.

Url, of Mitterlabill, southern Austria, rigged up a mitre saw and sliced off his foot – then put it in the oven for good measure to ensure no surgeon could reattach it.

But job centre staff have delivered a blow to hapless Url's plan by saying his new disability does not rule him out for work.

Police spokesman Franz Fasching said: 'The planning was meticulous.

'He waited until his wife and his adult son had left the house and he was alone.

'He then switched it on and sliced off his left foot above the ankle - throwing it in the fire so it would not be possible to reattach it before he called emergency services.

'He then made his way to the garage where he called emergency services and waited for them to arrive.

The police added that the man had almost died from loss of blood before the emergency services arrived and that they had recovered the foot from the oven - but that it had been too badly burned to reattach.

He was airlifted to hospital in Graz where his condition was said to be stable after emergency surgery to seal the wound.

A hospital spokesman said: 'The foot was too badly burned to reattach. All we could do was seal the wound. He had lost a lot of blood - he almost died on the way to hospital. He was put in an artificial coma.'

Url then threw his foot into this oven to make sure surgeons could not reattach it

The police spokesman Fasching added that they were investigating the case as an attempted suicide.

But Feldbach AMS job centre spokesman Hermann Gössinger said: 'This is a tragic case but it will not help the man.

'His latest excuse had been a bad back which is why he had been sent for a medical.

'But even now losing a foot does not automatically mean he will not be able to work. He will be assessed once he is out of hospital and we will see what work we can find for him.'

Source

The Huffington Post, 05/06/2012

Boris Cerni and Zachary Tracer, Bloomberg News

Tom Gardner, The Daily Mail, 27 March 2012

30

Corporate Welfare

Publicly Funded

Corporate profit is exaggerated by what is effectively publicly funded corporate welfare. The package of corporate welfare begins with governments who offer incentives to corporations in order to attract their business, increase their GDP and compete with other nations. National resources that rightfully belong to the public are the first carrots on the stick, and are offered at highly discounted prices to corporations without public consent. Governments even give away valuable common assets at no cost to corporations, such as oil and mineral rights, saving corporations billions of dollars in costs.

In addition, affluent governments pay out huge subsidies to the largest corporations. Government support to farmers in OECD countries totalled $283 billion in 2005, representing 29% of total farm income. Unfortunately, the majority of farmers who own small to medium sized farms do not benefit from these subsidies. 30% of farmers in the US do not receive any of the $26 billion of US subsidies, and over 85% go to only 20% of the largest farms, a pattern repeated in the EU.

Industrialized countries also subsidize corporate exports and agribusiness inputs such as energy, pesticides and chemical fertilizers. This encourages energy and chemical intensive production methods that only large scale agri-business can sustain. As a direct result, the number of small farms in the US has decreased from 6.8 million in 1935 to 1.5 million in 1998. In global commodity markets these subsidies mean that producers in developing countries, many of whom produce their goods with more efficiency and less cost than the US and EU, cannot compete with agri-business suppliers. Their livelihoods are destroyed. Market competition is cut throat, valued higher than life itself. Individual cows in Japan receive $8 a day in subsidies alone, whilst half of India's 1.2 billion people live on less than $2 a day. These actions strengthen the market dominance of corporations, whilst marginalizing smaller, community based producers.

In addition, corporations pay much less tax than ordinary people, often registering their headquarters in tax havens. According to the Centre for American Progress "At a time of rising corporate profits, the US Government Accountability Office (GAO) reports that 95 percent of corporations paid less than 5 percent of their income in taxes, and 6 in 10 paid nothing at all in federal taxes from 1996 through to 2000". The corporate share of taxes paid fell from 33 percent in the 1940's to 15 percent in the 1990's. The individual's share of taxes has risen from 44 to 73 percent. At a time of record corporate revenues, the American public is making up the loss in tax revenue through the government's biased tax regime.

The effect of corporate welfare upon the poorest nations is most disastrous. When local resources and basic goods are controlled by corporations and absentee owners, local industry is curbed, essential services are often unaffordable and profits are repatriated in wealthy countries, bypassing the local economy. Although privatization in developing countries does prove beneficial in certain cases, overall the process resembles economic mercantilism as it is ultimately fuelled by selfish, commercial interest. What is needed is a significant transfer of resources to the global south, not to multinational corporations.

When governments give away public resources, subsidize the largest industries and provide tax incentives to corporations, it usually occurs without the public's knowledge and proves detrimental to their local communities. The price we pay for goods does not include the cost we have already paid through our taxes, the cost to the poorest producers around the world, or the cost to the environment.

Cost Externalization

Classical economic thinking and accounting procedures are heavily biased against local communities and the environment, as they only reflect financial profit and loss. Maximizing profit means passing more immaterial or long-term costs on to society for them to deal with. This process is known as externalization, and externalities are typically negative social or environmental costs to a community, region or the planet which corporations do not have to account for in anyway. Corporations are compelled to externalize costs wherever possible so that they can increase their profits.

For example, export-oriented industrial agriculture is a major contributor to climate change. Agricultural externalities poison our soil, waterways and atmosphere. And corporations are learning to externalize more efficiently - they may, for example, relocate to countries with lower labour or environmental standards. The negative effect upon society and the environment of these externalities and lower standards are unaccounted for in the cost of their products or their financial reports. In the meantime, consumers are taken in by the illusion of low cost goods and services and they seek out ever cheaper suppliers. However, as the true environmental and social costs of corporate activity are becoming apparent, consumers must realize that they cannot avoid paying for them in one way or another. For example, these costs are paid through aid sent to developing countries (often after climate-change aggravated disasters); through the public money spent on tackling climate change; through the millions spent nationally tackling poverty, inequality, unemployment and other social issues; and through the detrimental effect upon quality of life that results from lower working standards and conditions.

Every year corporations are fined hundreds of millions of dollars as their externalities create serious environmental catastrophes, neglect employee rights and even cause deaths. Examples are plentiful and well documented by countless NGO and civil society groups, and usually concern the most well known and largest corporations. However, mainstream media coverage of these issues is virtually non existent. Take for example Chevron. The majority are unaware that it is guilty of some of the worst environmental and human rights abuses in the world such as the dumping of 18 billion gallons of toxic waste into rivers used for bathing water in the Amazon, devastating the health of the local community.

However, fines for these corporate crimes are negligible in relation to a company's turnover. The likelihood of being fined is often accounted for well before the event. Given the potential financial savings to be gained by violating environmental protection laws and workers rights, the decision to ignore these laws constitute a simple cost-benefit calculation. Worryingly, shareholders cannot be held accountable for these violations as they are protected by their limited liability, and directors and executives successfully plea that they have no direct involvement with the corporate crime committed. Thus the corporate 'entity' itself is fined, and little incentive to change irresponsible corporate behaviour is provided.

Taking the cost of these externalities into account, Ralph Estes estimated that the public cost of private corporations was over $3 trillion in 1995. His externalities included "workplace injuries, pollution, employment discrimination, consumer rip-offs, corporate white collar crime, tax abatements and all the other instances of corporate welfare, government contracting fraud and creative accounting" all of which have carry an equivalent financial cost to the public. Estes calculations reveal that the corporate claim to efficiency is clearly false - most corporations would not be able to continue without major changes if they bore the full costs of their of their product or service.

Conclusion

Clearly a corporation's pressing need for increased profits comes at too high a cost to the global public. When corporate welfare and the public cost of externalities are taken into account, corporate profit is a meaningless term. Within the current framework, corporate profit must be viewed alongside the social and environmental consequences of corporate activity. This more balanced approach calls into question the global economic system that perpetuates this state of affairs.

(Source: Multinational Corporations, STWR)

31

Patenting Life

Under the WTO's Agreement on Trade-Related Aspects of Intellectual Property Rights (TRIPS) agreement, the most insidious corporate victories to date have been the granting of patent protections to all genetic material. In 1980, the US Supreme Court ruled that a particular genetically engineered micro-organism could be patented. This patent right was extended by the US patent Office in 1985 to cover all genetically-engineered plants, seeds and plant tissue, and was further extended to cover all animals in 1987. In 1998 EU countries extended patent laws to cover patents on plants, humans and life forms.

Biotech companies are being snapped up by giant 'Life Science' corporations in a race to consolidate the food and seeds industry which tripled in size between 1992 and 2002. It was worth around $2,000 billion

Discussions regarding economic systems should not be based on ideologies of socialism or capitalism, but on the practicalities and realities of our modern world. Today, the reality is that thousands will die from a lack of food, water and medicine, because of the failure of the global economy to allow them to have access to these basics. At the same time, a few business people will have earned millions of dollars in wages, thanks to the same economic system. These extremes must be reconciled urgently.

a year in 2001. By May 2002, there were 1,457 biotechnology companies in the US with a total value of $224 billion. Market consolidation is acute, 70% of patents on staple food crops are held by six multinational corporations who can set the market price for them and block competition for 20 years, thereby monopolizing the market.

Patenting costs can be up to $1 million, ensuring that those in the developing countries cannot possibly compete with the wealthy corporations. The developing world, where 75% of people's livelihoods depend upon agriculture, is the source of 90 per cent of all biological resources. Yet transnational companies based in developed counties hold 97 percent of global patents. Since 1985 there have been 10,778 patents on plants registered in the US. Overall, patent applications at the World Intellectual Property Organization have soared from 3,000 in 1979 to 67,000 in 1997.

Commercially owned genetic varieties of such staples as cotton and soya beans have devastated farming communities in developing countries, who can no longer store seeds without paying corporations for the privilege. There has been widespread opposition to what has been deemed 'bio piracy'. This is when biotechnology corporations,

The Global Economy

Corporations should exist as an integral component of a global economy that prioritizes the provision of basic needs for the global public – economic, social, political and spiritual. The primary objective of the global economy should not be commerce, trade liberalization or economic growth, but the production and distribution of all resources that are essential to life. International consensus must eventually lead to a clear demarcation with regards to what can be commoditized and what cannot be.

in their haste to secure financial advantages, patent varieties of plants, seeds and applications that already exist and remain in use by indigenous communities. The patenting of life goes against the sharing of traditional knowledge and the preservation of biodiversity and culture. This precedent is a major victory for corporations. The potential for future profit is almost limitless.

(Source: Rajesh Makwana, STWR, October 2006)

32

No Peace By Day

No Sleep At Night

Discrepancy Between 'What The Body Tells And What Boss Tells Us'.

Many workers get fewer than six hours of sleep each night, putting themselves and their co-workers at risk for serious and sometimes deadly consequences, according to federal health officials.

"There about 41 million US workers who aren't getting the recommended amount of sleep," says Dr. Sara Luckhaupt, lead author of a new study from the division of surveillance, hazard evaluations and field studies at the National Institute for Occupational Safety and Health. The institute is part of the U.S. Centers for Disease Control and Prevention.

"Not surprisingly, workers who work the night shift are more likely to not get enough sleep," she said. Also, people who work more than one job or more than 40 hours a week are likely to get too little sleep", Luckhaupt says.

The National Sleep Foundation recommends that adults sleep six to eight hours a night.

About 44 percent of night shift workers get too little sleep, compared to about 29 percent of people working the day shift. And certain industries take more of a toll on sleep than hours. Nearly 70 percent of those working night shifts in transportation and warehousing are sleep-deprived, the study says.

Working nights and sleeping during the day, in particular, disrupts the natural sleep cycle, called circadian rhythm. Workers who don't get enough sleep are more likely to get injured on the job and make mistakes that could injure them and their co-workers, according to the report.

Over time, insufficient sleep can also affect overall health, resulting in cardiovascular problems, obesity, diabetes and depression.

But there are way employers can help workers get enough sleep, such as not starting shifts too early in the morning. If shifts rotate, it is better to go from an evening shift to a night shift than the other way around.

Employees can also promote good sleep habits. These include going to sleep at the same time every day, having the bedroom quiet, dark and not too hot or too cold, and using the bed for sleep, not for reading or watching TV.

For the report, published in the April 27, 2012 issue of the CDC's Morbidity and Mortality Weekly Report, researchers used data from the 2010 National Health Interview Survey to assess sleep habits of American workers.

Shelby Freedman Harris, director of the Behavioral Sleep Medicine Program and the Sleep-Wake Disorders Center at Montefiore Medical Center in New York City, says that "our society is a very sleep-deprived one."

The results are worrisome, he says, and include increased risk of heart attack, stroke, falls, car accidents, poor attention, depression, work absenteeism, irritability and weight gain.

"Despite these consequences, many people still don't find the time for adequate sleep, with many having trouble with insomnia and not seeking proper help," he adds.

There are effective treatments to help with sleep issues arising from rotating shift work issues, but many people are unaware of them and many companies are not implementing them.

For those working overnight shifts, strategically using bright light before and during work hours is helpful, along with dimming the lights at the end of the work period and wearing sunglasses on the drive home, he says.

For some workers, planning out a nap schedule is key. Others may require restructuring their sleep times at home.

"I strongly encourage anyone who is struggling with adjusting to their shift to consult with a specialist. What is also important is making sure you have enough time between shifts to obtain a full night's sleep -- something many companies don't necessarily allow for," Harris says.

Snoozing At Your Desk? Piling On The Pounds? You May Have Social Jetlag

People's health is suffering because of discrepancy between 'what the body tells and what boss tells us'. It could be key factor behind obesity epidemic and bad habits like smoking and drinking

Our hectic lifestyles and demanding jobs have left many of us battling 'social jetlag', researchers say.

It is caused by a mismatch between the body's internal clock – which says we should get up when it becomes light and go to sleep

I was taking over the counter sleeping tablets for over a year and about 6 weeks ago they started to become less effective and that's when the withdrawel symptons started. I had constant severe anxiety, waves of panic attacks and clinical depression. My Dr gave me diazapam and zopiclone to help me cope with the withdrawel symptons. I'm over the worst and off all the tablets but still feel mentally fragile. I thought the over the counter sleeping tablets were non addictive and had very few side affects but the Dr said that any sleeping tablet should only be used short term because they will cause more harm than good to you in the long run. After feeling that i've had a glimpse of hell these past few weeks i never want to take another sleeping pill again.
~ Jayne, Wales. UK

when it gets dark – and the realities of our daily work and social schedules.

Doctor Till Roenneberg, of the University of Munich in Germany, said: 'We have identified a syndrome in modern society that has not been recognised until recently.

'It concerns an increasing discrepancy between the daily timing of the physiological clock and the social clock.

'As a result of this social jetlag, people are chronically sleep-deprived. They are also more likely to smoke and drink more alcohol and caffeine.

'Now, we show that social jetlag also contributes to obesity; the plot that social jetlag is really bad for our health is thickening.'

He explained that every human has a biological clock, but we can't set the clock according to our whims like watches.

They are rather regulated by daylight and darkness to provide the optimal window for sleep and waking.

Dr Roenneberg said: 'In modern society, we listen to those clocks less and less due to the increasing discrepancy between what the body clock tells us and what the boss tells us.'

'He's tired – he was up all night worring about his sleeping pill consumption'

To find out the scale of the problem, Dr Roenneberg's team is compiling a vast database on human sleeping and waking behaviour, which they'll eventually use to produce a world sleep map.

Now, 10 years into the effort, they already have lots of information - including participants' height, weight, and sleep patterns.

Their analysis shows that people with more severe social jetlag are also more likely to be overweight.

Dr Roenneberg said, in other words, it appears that living 'against the clock' may be a factor contributing to the epidemic of obesity.

He said it would help if people began spending more time outdoors in open daylight or at least sitting by a window. A good night's sleep is not a luxury but essential to having a happy and healthy work and social life.

As people fail to do so for one reason or another, their body clocks get set later and later, leaving them awake into the night and tired by day.

Dr Roenneberg added: 'Waking up with an alarm clock is a relatively new facet of our lives.

'It simply means that we haven't slept enough and this is the reason why we are chronically tired.

'Good sleep and enough sleep is not a waste of time but a guarantee for better work performance and more fun with friends and family during off-work times.'

The findings were published in the journal Current Biology.

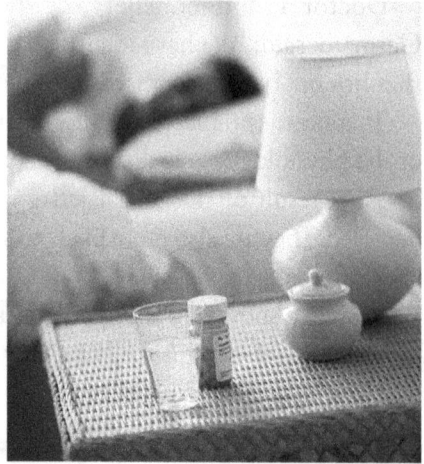

A couple of weeks ago my marriage suffered a major blip after 24 years, & one of the worst results of this was that I simply could not sleep. At all. This was just so debilitating – I couldn't work, I couldn't think straight, I couldn't drive., I could barely even hold a conversation. In the end I went to my Doctor & got some pills which have worked really well for me. In 10 days I have taken them 3 times, but I know they are there if I need them. Never underestimate sleep deprivation – it is horrific to live with.
~ Henley, London

Addiction To Sleeping Pills: Stress-Related Insomnia On The Rise

There is alarming rise in the number of sleeping pill addicts since the start of the economic downturn.

Stress-related insomnia has been blamed for a sharp increase in the number of people prescribed powerful drugs to help them sleep.

In Britain alone, the annual cost to the NHS of handing out the pills has risen by a sixth in the past three years to nearly £50million.

But there are fears that strong medication is being given out too readily and patients are becoming hooked.

Many of the most commonly used pills have potentially dangerous side effects including liver problems, headaches and nausea.

In UK, studies reveal a third of adults suffer from insomnia, while more than half say they still feel tired when they wake.

So this materialistic way of life is not human life. It is less than animal life. Animal also does not work so hard. You see? And the people are engaged, wherever you go, the very big highways. What is called? Freeways. Four lines of motor cars running this way and four lines of motor cars running this way at the speed of seventy miles, and everyone is busy. You see? And they take, "It is a very good civilization." And if you shortcut your hard labor, sit down and discuss what is the Absolute Truth, what is the philosophy of life, "They are nonsense." You see? And if you work day and night, hard labor, and to get that energy, inject some medicine or some tranquilizer and this and that... You see? This is going on. So actually, this is not life. This is cats' and dogs' life. That is the verdict of Srimad-Bhagavatam. Nayam deho deha-bhajam nr-loke kastan kaman arhate vid-bhujam ye: [SB 5.5.1] "This life, human form of life, is not meant for working so hard just like animals." Then? "This kind of engagement is for the dogs and hogs." The hogs also, they work the whole day and night and have some sex pleasure. They are happy. So is that life, simply working day and night hard and enjoy some sex pleasure some way or other, and we are thinking happy? No. This is not life. Life is to utilize the energy for perpetual happiness. They do not know that there is some perpetual happiness, there is perpetual life.

~ Srila Prabhupada (Srimad-Bhagavatam 7.9.8 -- Hawaii, March 21, 1969)

Figures obtained from health trusts under a freedom of information request reveal that last year 15.3million prescriptions were handed out for sleeping pills, compared with 14.5million in 2007/8.

Last year the NHS spent £49.2million on such drugs, up from £42million three years previously. This is an increase of more than 17 per cent.

Dr Andrew McCulloch, chief executive of the Mental Health Foundation, said: 'The most likely explanation is the increase in stress-related insomnia.

'We are seeing an increase in people presenting with a range of issues including anxiety, depression and general stress-related complaints.

'There's a significant increase in stress-related problems caused by the economic environment. This might be due to unemployment, debt or just general doom and gloom in society.

'Most sleep problems are caused by stress and anxiety, although some are caused by chronic pain or sleep apnoea,' he added.

Mandeep Mudhar, NHS business director at the Co-operative Pharmacy, which obtained the figures, said: 'Our research shows that millions of people suffer from a lack of sleep each year and are seeking medical help for the problem.

'While usage has risen steadily, the costs to the NHS have risen disproportionately, with costs going up at a greater rate. However some sleeping drugs are only recommended for short-term use because they can lead to psychological dependency and lose their effectiveness over time.

'Sleep patterns can be affected by physical or psychological factors and the continued economic downturn is a likely cause for the increased use of sleeping pills because of the heightened stress, anxiety and worry levels people face as a result of job insecurity or money worries.'

Last year a survey of 5,300 adults found that 61 per cent did not always get a good night's sleep. The British Sleep Study, carried out by the Mental Health Foundation, also found that 37 per cent had insomnia with another 24 per cent having sleep apnoea or teeth-grinding.

Insomnia is defined as having sleep disturbances on at least three nights a week which lead to problems the next day.

Researchers also found that insomnia sufferers were four times more likely to suffer relationship problems. Some 55 per cent had difficulties with their partners compared to 13 per cent who slept well.

They are three times more likely to lack concentration during the day and more than twice as likely to suffer from low energy.

Other studies have linked lack of sleep to obesity. Last month academics from Boston calculated that getting less than five and a half hours sleep a night caused people to gain a stone a year because their metabolism would slow down.

Source
Steven Reinberg, The Daily Mail, April 27, 2012
Chris Hanlon, Health Day Reporter, 10 May 2012
Sophie Borland, The Daily Mail, 10 May 2012

33

Lobbying

The Prime Corporate Pastime

In his exhaustive book, 'When Corporations Rule the World', David Korten identifies the Council of Foreign Relations, the Bilderberg and the Trilateral Commission as key historical institutions that shaped modern economic globalization.

These well funded, highly influential and often rather secretive institutions, brought together key government ministers, business leaders, educators and media representatives as early as 1939.

Together they created the necessary consensus for economic globalization and shaped public opinion to support the policies that were essential to their goal.

Eighty percent of all corporations reside in the US and EU, and through their lobbyists they enjoy privileged access to the government policy makers who partake in trade talks. Over 30,000 corporate lobbyists are based in Washington and Brussels, vastly outnumbering the US Congress and European Commission staff that they lobby.

The result of association with the qualities of passion and ignorance is that one becomes lusty and greedy. But when one is elevated to the platform of goodness, he is satisfied in any condition of life and is without lust and greed. This mentality indicates one's situation on the platform of goodness.
~ Srila Prabhupada (Srimad Bhagavatam 4.21.52)

The vast majority of lobby groups represent business interests who spend billions of dollars annually advocating their main cause, which is currently market access in emerging economies. In the US, corporations and their agencies spent $9.7 billion lobbying Congress between 1997 and 2000, about $4.5 million per year per member of Congress.

On the other hand, many developing countries do not have the resources to send enough, if any, representatives to argue for fairer trade practices that would benefit their own economic development. In addition, WTO negotiations are undemocratic, with the public denied access to, or information about, the discussions. The same is not true of corporate lobby groups such as the European Services Forum (ESF) and many US corporations who can directly affect and have access to Trade Committees.

Unsurprisingly then, the interests of rich nations and their corporations form the basis of WTO agreements and directly influence the global political and economic architecture. The corporate bottom line, espoused by the WTO, is to open market access in all countries to resources, services and intellectual property in an endless drive for greater profits.

Corporate Links to Government

In his book Captive State (2000), George Monbiot lists 43 individuals who, since the 1997 elections in the UK, have been appointed as ministers, heads, chairmen, and advisors to as many government departments and independent committees. In each case their previous corporate positions (mostly as directors, chairmen or chief executives) and existing links to industry present a direct conflict of interest with their governmental roles.

Large swathes of Africa, Asia and South America do not have the resources to compete internationally even if the terms of trade were rendered fair and their debts forgiven. Within a system of sharing, resources that are considered essential to life would not be commoditized or controlled by business interests.

To take a random example, Lord Simon of Highbury, the previous chairman of oil giant BP and vice chairman of the European Roundtable of industrialists (a powerful corporate lobby group) was appointed minister for Trade and Competitiveness in Europe at the Department of Trade and Industry.

As expected, the same conflict of interest exists at the highest levels in the US government, only more openly and to greater detriment. The majority of President Bush's cabinet were multimillionaires. The President, Vice-President, Commerce Secretary and National Security Adviser all had strong ties to the oil industry. The Bush family had strong ties to Enron-which was President G. W. Bush's largest corporate source of funding.

Condoleezza Rice was a director of Chevron. Secretary of Commerce Donald Evans held stock valued between $5m and $25m in Tom Brown Inc, the oil and gas exploration company he headed, and the list goes on, highlighting in particular a pronounced concentration of energy connections.

Unsurprisingly, US domestic and foreign policies are highly biased. The securing of Iraqi oil fields is a pertinent recent example. Since the beginning of the Iraq war, Halliburton, the Texas energy giant once headed by Vice President Dick Cheney, has seen its stock price more than triple in value. According to Halliburton Watch, Halliburton's contracts under the Bush administration grew by 600%.

tvam vartamanam nara-deva-dehesv
anupravrtto 'yam adharma-pugah
lobho 'nrtam cauryam anaryam amho
jyestha ca maya kalahas ca dambhah

If the personality of Kali, irreligion, is allowed to act as a man-god or an executive head, certainly irreligious principles like greed, falsehood, robbery, incivility, treachery, misfortune, cheating, quarrel and vanity will abound. This kind of government cannot check the resultant actions of sinful life, namely war, pestilence, famine, earthquakes and similar other disturbances.

~ Srila Prabhupada (Srimad Bhagavatam 1.17.32)

To take a key aspect of the administration's tax plan, Bush's cabinet members, according to one estimate, saved between $5 million and $19 million each as the Bush administration repealed the Estate Tax. This will come at the cost of an estimated $1 trillion dollars over the first 10 years to the public.

Those who benefited from the tax cuts represent a fraction of 1% of the American public. It is this same elite section of US citizens that dominate and manipulate the entire political system. As such, a symbiotic relationship is established, with both the government and the corporate elite sustaining each others legitimacy.

Winning Elections

Money is equated with political influence within global governance structures. Raising massive contributions for campaign spending is only open to those with very strong connections to wealthy individuals. Civil society simply cannot compete financially, and the current state of politics reflects this situation. This misused financial leverage and influence is also at the heart of global governance injustice. The IMF and World Bank operate on a 'one

Is it not the desire to uphold outmoded systems of commerce and economy, based on competition and selfish, nationalistic foreign policy objectives, which is truly reactionary and conservative?

The need for far reaching reform of business structure and activity is apparent, as is the need for democratic participation to be re-established at the community level. Economic development must be a process which is not imposed from above, but secured locally, and then regionally. For this to occur, all necessary resources should be made available to the majority world who mainly live in isolated, rural communities in developing countries. We have a United Nations General Assembly, the only world body with the potential to bring about these reforms. We also have the technology to implement complex systems that can span the globe, and we have the infrastructure and capability to distribute resources anywhere. All this is required is a shift in priorities; the political will to share what we have.

dollar, one vote' basis, denying the democratic rights of the majority of the world simply because they are not wealthy enough.

In US, corporations were allowed to finance elections in the mid 1970's when the US Supreme Court extended First Amendment Constitutional Rights to corporations, allowing them an extension of 'free speech' rights originally intended for people. The 2004 US presidential elections were the most expensive ever; total campaign contributions were $880,500,000.

Even in the 2002 Congressional races, where money was much less a determinant of the victors than the 2000 elections, 95% of all House seats and 75% of Senate seats were won by the higher-spending candidate.

The coal industry donated $1.5 million during the 2002 election cycle, mostly to the Republicans, Enron gave $2 million between 1999 and 2002, and Eli Lilly and Company gave over $1 million. In return for these and countless other contributions, President Bush's policies during his administration clearly favoured the wealthy and corporate interests by awarding lucrative contracts and by adjusting policy and laws.

Reference

Kaufmann, Daniel and Pedro Vicente, 2011, Legal Corruption, Economics and Politics.

Penelope Patsuris (26 August 2002), The Corporate Scandal Sheet, Forbes.

Braithwaite, John. (1984). Corporate Crime in the Pharmaceutical Industry. London: Routledge & Kegan Paul Books.

Mokhiber, Russell & Weissmann, Robert. (1999). Corporate Predators : The Hunt for Mega-Profits and the Attack on Democracy. Common Courage Press.

Clinard, Marshall B. & Yeager, Peter Cleary. (2005). Corporate Crime. Somerset, NJ: Transaction Publishers.

34

We're Now So Busy

We Don't Even Have Time To Taste The Food We Eat

79% unable to identify basic flavours, survey found

People are losing touch with their taste buds because of the pace of modern life, researchers claim.

A survey found that 60 per cent of those polled admitted to never or rarely tasting what they eat.

In tests, 79 per cent were unable to tell the difference between basic flavours.

The figure rose to 88 per cent when people were distracted, and 93 per cent when they came under time pressure.

Just 13 per cent of people questioned said they had lunch away from their workplace, and almost half described the midday meal as 'a means to an end' to refuel the body.

Psychologist David Lewis, from the Mindlab consultancy, said: 'The abundance of great flavours and the range of food experiences have never been more plentiful in the UK, nor more diverse, yet our findings suggest consumers are lazy when it comes to tasting and appreciating their food.

'I doubt there's ever been such a rich tapestry of food and flavour combinations at our disposal, yet we're not savouring what we eat, which is not just a shame but a genuine waste of taste.

'Our lunchtime habits in particular show that workers consume food as a means to refuelling the body and almost never, or rarely, taste what they're eating.'

A total of 1,000 people took part in the survey, with a small sub-group of 30 volunteering to take the taste tests.

In the tests, participants were given a range of eight sandwiches and asked to identify the ingredients. A number of the sandwiches were deliberately mislabelled.

Volunteers were able to identify 35 per cent of the ingredients correctly.

In addition, 93 per cent were unable to distinguish between beef and Chinese pork, 92 per cent could not tell ham from tuna, 82 per cent were confused by Quorn and chicken, and 78 per cent mistook pork for chicken and vice versa.

The survey and tests were commissioned by soup and sauce makers Glorious.

Dr Lewis urged people to eat 'mindfully' without rushing, while avoiding distractions such as TV.

'Mindless eating means that the food goes down so rapidly that by the time the stomach signals to the brain that it has 'had enough' we have, in fact, overeaten,' he said.

'The consequence is that we add unnecessary calories and so put on weight.'

When people are not even conscious of the food they are eating, how can they be conscious of the animals that have been killed to

Now I get it! Thats how stores are able to get away with selling those 'healthy option' sandwiches. Busy people don't notice thay taste of cardboard! Clever!

- Jackie, Bristol, 21/5/2012

prepare that food. They are acting more like mechanical zombies than sensible human beings.

Busy Bees -Arranging To Meet Friends Can Take Weeks

The average citizen in countries like Britain is now so busy they have to make plans five weeks in advance simply to meet up with friends, according to a new research.

Figures reveal one in ten of our dairies are now packed for the next ten weeks with work commitments, kids' parties, christenings and family weekends.

That means no spare time for the next 2 months. And the average Brit already has plans to attend at least three weddings next year.

The study, by hotel chain Premier Inn, found 25 per cent enjoy having a full diary, while 50 per cent plan in advance to ensure they've got something to look forward to.

But a further 15 per cent said they felt pressured to fill up spare weekends because they didn't want to waste them.

And 31 per cent are so desperate to have time to themselves they now admit finding excuses to avoid making plans with friends and family.

Claire Haigh, from Premier Inn, said: 'These days people are busier than ever.

'With more and more weekend commitments stacking up, even simply arranging to meet a friend for a drink can take weeks.

'Many are now realising that time is precious and we don't want to waste a minute, so making back-to-back plans is often the only way to combat this.'

Source:
The Daily Mail Reporter, 21 May 2012
Maysa Rawi, The Daily Mail, 13 March 2012

35

Epidemic Of 'Sickness Presenteeism'

Workers 'Too Scared To Go Off Sick'

The recession has fuelled a widespread paranoia among workers who are 'too scared' about losing their jobs to take time off work when they are sick, official figures revealed recently.

The Office for National Statistics in UK said the average number of sick days taken by workers has dropped to the lowest number since records began in 1993.

Since the recession began in 2008, the average number of sick days has fallen every single year to the current all-time low of just 4.5 days per year.

In 1993, the average was 7.2 days. By 2007 - the year before the recession began - it was 5.6 days, but has fallen each year from 5.3 to 5 to 4.7 and, most recently, to 4.5 last year.

Experts today said many workers are not taking off a single day all year, even if they get struck down by an illness which would usually leave them in bed for a week.

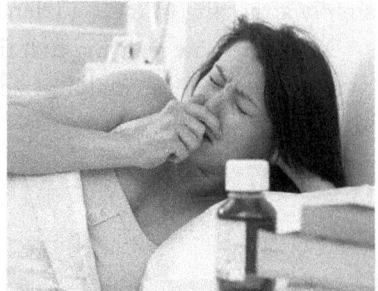

Professor Cary Cooper, from the Lancaster University Management School, said: 'People are too scared to take time off.

'Even if they are ill, they are coming into work. It is called "sickness presenteeism".

'Do you think anybody wants to have a bad sickness absence record with the boss at the current time?'

It comes as a time when unemployment has ballooned to 2.65 million, with more than 170,000 extra people over the last year desperately searching for a job but failing to find one.

The problem would be even worse if many unemployed people were not accepting part-time jobs because they could not find full-time employment.

Brendan Barber, general secretary of the Trades Union Congess, said: 'The biggest problem workplaces face is not absenteeism but "presenteeism" where workers come in when they are too ill.

'Presenteeism can multiply problems by making someone ill for longer and spreading germs around the workplace.'

Primitive means very, very old. So whether in the days gone by, people were actually happy or now they are happy?

Even if you say "primitive," the primitive life is very nice. Primitive life means simple life. Keeping pace with the nature's law. It is very nice. Primitive life ... It gives you anxiety-free life, and therefore, even if you take it as primitive, the saintly persons, sages, they used to live long, long years, and their brain was so sharp, because they were taking natural food, fruits, grains, and milk that helps to develop human brain for understanding subtle subject matter. So even Vyasadeva... You have seen the picture of Vyasadeva. He's writing books just near a cottage only. But he's writing. Nobody can create such literature. But he was leading very simple life, in a cottage. Even, say, 2,000 years ago or little more, there was Canakya Pandita. Canakya Pandita, he was a brahmana, but great politician. His politics are studied even now in M.A. class.

~Srila Prabhupada (Lecture, Srimad-Bhagavatam 2.3.24, Los Angeles, June 22, 1972)

Professor Cooper added: 'People are feeling so insecure about their job that, even when they are ill, they are going to come to work. 'The last thing in the world that they need is redundancy.'

In a sign of the extreme presenteeism culture in Britain, the news that the chief executive of Lloyds was timing time off work due to exhaustion last year caused widespread shock.

Antonio Horta-Osorio, who returned to work in January, later described how he would 'go to bed exhausted but could not get to sleep', adding: 'I could not switch off.'

The Portugese-born boss, who spent a week in mental health clinic the Priory, said the gruelling experience meant he now understood why sleep deprivation is used to torture prisoners.

Source
Becky Barrow, The Daily Mail, 15 May 2012
Sara Smyth, The Daily Mail, 4 May 2013

36

Missing Out On Life

Impoverishment Of The Human Spirit

A man sat at a metro station in Washington DC and started to play the violin; it was a cold January morning. He played six Bach pieces for about 45 minutes. During that time, since it was rush hour, it was calculated that 1,100 people went through the station, most of them on their way to work.

Three minutes went by, and a middle aged man noticed there was musician playing. He slowed his pace, and stopped for a few seconds, and then hurried up to meet his schedule.

A minute later, the violinist received his first dollar tip: a woman threw the money in the till and without stopping, and continued to walk.

A few minutes later, someone leaned against the wall to listen to him, but the man looked at his watch and started to walk again. Clearly he was late for work.

The one who paid the most attention was a 3 year old boy. His mother tagged him along, hurried, but the kid stopped to look at the

> *Driving at breakneck speed. And then what is the business? Searching out some means of food, exactly like the hog, he is loitering here and there, "Where is stool? Where is stool? Where is stool?" And this is going on in the polished way as civilization. There is so much risk, as running these cars so many people are dying. There is record, it is very dangerous. At least I feel as soon as I go to the street, it is dangerous. The motorcar are running so speedy, and what is the business? The business is where to find out food. So therefore it is condemned that this kind of civilization is hoggish civilization. This hog is running after, "Where is stool? And you are running in a car. Purpose is the same: Therefore this is not advancement of civilization. Advancement of civilization is, as Krsna advises, that you require food, so produce food grain. Remain wherever you are. You can produce food grain anywhere, a little labor. And keep cows, go-raksya, krsi-go-raksya vanijyam vaisya-karma svabhava-jam [Bg. 18.44]. Solve your problem like... Produce your food wherever you are there. Till little, little labor, and you will get your whole year's food. And distribute the food to the animal, cow, and eat yourself. The cow will eat the refuse. You take the rice, and the skin you give to the cow. From dahl you take the grain, and the skin you give to the... And fruit, you take the fruit, and the skin you give to the cow, and he will give you milk. So why should you kill her? Milk is the miraculous food; therefore Krsna says cow protection. Give protection to the cow, take milk from it, and eat food grains -- your food problem is solved. Where is food problem? Why should you invent such civilization always full of anxieties, running the car here and there, and fight with other nation, and economic development? What is this civilization?*
> *— Srila Prabhupada (Philosophical discussion)*

violinist. Finally, the mother pushed hard, and the child continued to walk, turning his head all the time. This action was repeated by several other children. All the parents, without exception, forced them to move on.

In the 45 minutes the musician played, only 6 people stopped and stayed for a while. About 20 gave him money, but continued to walk their normal pace. He collected $32. When he finished playing and silence took over, no one noticed it. No one applauded, nor was there any recognition.

No one knew this, but the violinist was Joshua Bell, one of the most talented musicians in the world. He had just played one of the most intricate pieces ever written, on a violin worth $3.5 million dollars.

Two days before his playing in the subway, Joshua Bell sold out at a theater in Boston where the seats averaged $100.

This is a real story. Joshua Bell playing incognito in the metro station was organized by the Washington Post as part of a social experiment about perception, taste, and priorities of people. The outlines were: in a commonplace environment at an inappropriate hour: Do we perceive beauty? Do we stop to appreciate it? Do we recognize the talent in an unexpected context?

One of the possible conclusions from this experience could be:

If we do not have a moment to stop and listen to one of the best musicians in the world playing the best music ever written, how many other things are we missing?"

Source
David Emery, A Violinist in the Metro, Netlore Archive, Dec. 17, 2008
Brett M. Christensen, The Hoax-Slayer, 8th January 2009

37

Make A Bold Dash For Freedom

Downshifting or Voluntary Simplicity

To escape the clutches of corporate world is not easy as they have their tentacles spread in all directions. Many people are quitting main stream city life to relocate themselves on the land. Some are opting out of the rat race by voluntarily accepting a simpler life.

When one voluntarily decides to consume less, it is called voluntary simplicity. Voluntary simplicity means doing/having/living more with less - more time, more meaning, more joy, satisfaction, relationships, community; less money, less material possessions, less stress, competition, isolation. Voluntary simplicity is a growing movement of people who have realized that happiness and fulfillment do not lie in having more money, or new and bigger things.

So in this type of lifestyle individuals consciously choose to minimize the 'more-is-better' pursuit of wealth and consumption. Adherents choose simple living for a variety of reasons, including spirituality, health, increase in 'quality time' for family and friends, stress reduction, conservation, social justice or anti-consumerism, while others choose to live more simply for reasons of personal taste or personal economy.

Simple living as a concept is distinguished from those living in forced poverty, as it is a voluntary lifestyle choice. Although asceticism resembles voluntary simplicity, proponents of simple living are not all ascetics. The term "downshifting" is often used to describe the act of moving from a lifestyle of greater consumption towards a lifestyle based on voluntary simplicity.

The act of voluntary simplicity or cultivation of detachment has been the focal point of all religious teachings. In human history, there have been countless souls who led a life of selflessness, dedication and voluntary simplicity. These personalities are respected, revered and remembered even today.

Also known as downshifting, many today are deciding to reduce their incomes and place family, friends and contentment above money in determining their life goals.

Voluntary Simplicity - From Fast Track Fast Food To Slow Track Slow Food Life

As the following article shows, there is a movement toward "Voluntary Creative Simplicity." It appeared in The Sun on January 2, 2008.

How We Went From $42,000 To $6,500 And Lived To Tell About It!

By L. Kevin & Donna Philippe-Johnson

As a middle class American, it's been difficult for me to understand how we are supposed to make a living when there are so many things working against us. How can we go on day after day with the rising cost of food, fuel, utilities, car insurance, taxes and health care, while dealing with the insecurity of unemployment? In the past, whenever I considered these things, I felt a hopeless sense of impending doom in the pit of my stomach. There is so much talk about how to solve these issues, but nothing ever seems to stop the downward spiral of struggle and stress that millions of folks are experiencing.

Like many working people, my life went along fine during the 1980s. I had a good paying job ($42,000 a year) and though I didn't enjoy the kind of work I was doing as an industrial draftsman, receiving a steady paycheck every week kept me going without much complaint. But then came the Gulf War in the 1990s and after that point I faced nine layoffs over the span of 10 years. By the time September 11 happened, I hadn't been able to maintain steady employment in the petrochemical industry for over a decade.

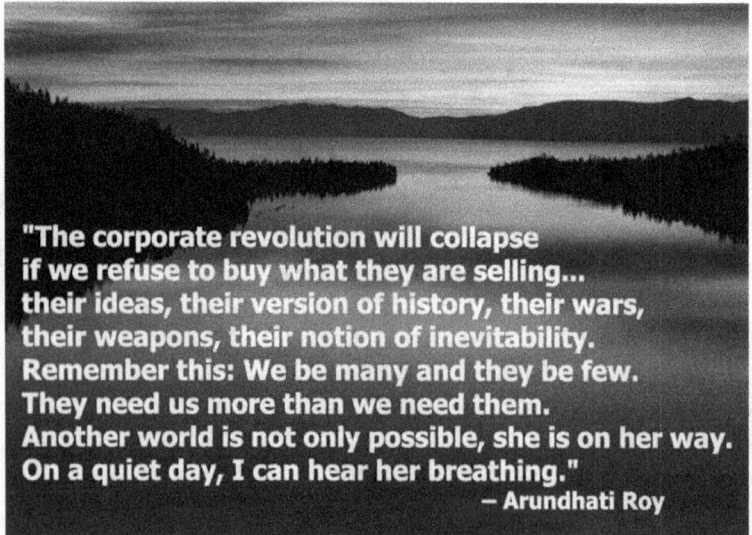

"The corporate revolution will collapse
if we refuse to buy what they are selling...
their ideas, their version of history, their wars,
their weapons, their notion of inevitability.
Remember this: We be many and they be few.
They need us more than we need them.
Another world is not only possible, she is on her way.
On a quiet day, I can hear her breathing."
— Arundhati Roy

I would work about three or four months, then back again to the unemployment line.

It was at this point that I realized that something was wrong. The life strategy I had grown up to believe in was no longer working and there didn't seem to be any answers. Obviously no one was going to get me out of this, so I decided I needed to take matters into my own hands and figure out a way to redefine my basic approach to living.

Lucky for me, I have an adventurous wife. She was on the same page with me and was willing to make some drastic changes in our lifestyle. As a committed team, we decided to figure out another way to survive despite these uncertain, hard economic times. Since we didn't have a lot of money and because it was getting harder to find steady employment, we decided to rethink our basic values in order to create a life for ourselves where we could be independent and free of needing a career or a full-time job.

And for us, that meant first and foremost, moving to the country. If we were going to be poor, we thought, at least it would be better to be poor in the country. That way we could grow our own food and reduce our expenses. Eventually we discovered that there were others who felt the same way we did. Today there is a small, but growing movement in this country towards a lifestyle we call "Voluntary Creative Simplicity."

We decided to start over, to shake loose from all the things holding us down. We got rid of all the stuff we didn't need and worked on paying off debt. Then canceling our credit cards and using cash, we followed an efficient financial plan that taught how to track every penny. By doing this we were able eventually to save a little bit of money.

Also, we wanted to be strong and healthy to do the work required for this basic lifestyle so we changed our eating habits. We broke away from the standard American fast food, pre-packaged supermarket diet in favor of organically grown whole grains, raw fruits and vegetables, fermented dairy, nuts, seeds and sprouts and eliminated all junk foods and prescription drugs. We started exercising regularly by walking, practicing yoga, and gardening. Since we no longer wanted to pay health insurance premiums, we decided to start a special savings account ($1,000) just for emergency first-aid treatment. And of course we got rid of the cell phone, cable television and Internet bills and greatly minimized our use of air conditioning. The beginning of the path to the simple life was a process of elimination in every aspect of our lives.

Eventually we found 2-1/2 acres of land, 35 miles out of the city. Inspired by our new vision, one summer we said goodbye to the city, permanently moved out to our new place and set up a dome tent to live in. We happily lived in our tent that summer while clearing the land and constructing a rustic 10' by 12' room with a sleeping loft. We did this on a "pay-as-you-go" plan, hauling all the materials in the back of our old pickup truck. Never having built anything before, we worked hard and gained the skill of building our own shelter.

As the tiny outbuilding took shape, next came the installation of an underground cistern for collecting rainwater, and finally, the construction of our three-room (500 square foot) cabin. Since we had to borrow $9,000 to purchase the property, I continued to take whatever jobs I could find (drafting, clerk work, courier, dishwasher, bakery assistant, etc.) while Donna (my wife!) stayed busy working on our organic garden, planting fruit trees and composting. She enjoys learning about native plants and healing herbs that she can grow.

Over the next few years, while working toward our goals of self-reliance and independence, we became stronger, healthier and more confident in our ability to rely on our own skills. It was quite an empowering experience. We learned how to build things, grow our own food, take responsibility for our own health, and best of all, we learned how to laugh and have fun again. The simple joys and true pleasures of fresh, home-grown food, watching everything grow and prosper in harmony, working with our own hands and spending quality time together replaced all of the costly false values that had occupied our time before.

Gradually we paid off the land, finished the cabin and succeeded in minimizing our basic utility costs. We began to notice that our expenses were decreasing as the quality of our life was increasing. As long as we stayed home and didn't travel to a steady job we really didn't need very much money. The lifestyle of voluntary creative simplicity was resulting in compounding efficiency and improvement in every area of our lives.

Soon, we saw the proof of the inefficiency of working a full-time job. After figuring in the work-related expenses of one job, I realized that my take home pay was only $3 an hour! At that point I was convinced that it was far more cost effective to stay home, grow our own food, split our own firewood and bake our own bread than it was to travel to a job day after day. Yet we still needed some form of income.

Though we had reduced the amount we needed to around $540 a month (way below the poverty level in America), we still had to find a way to generate that income without relying on full-time employment. Once we had succeeded in drastically reducing the amount of money we needed, I knew it would be easy to earn this income by working odd jobs such as building rustic furniture, playing guitar for tips, simple carpentry, part-time drafting, office work, plumbing, etc. However, there was one thing I really loved to do...bake handmade whole-grain sourdough bread in an outdoor wood-fired clay oven! I had always shared my bread with friends and family, but it never really occurred to me to do it as a way to earn extra money.

We soon discovered that there was no authentic, handmade sourdough bread being produced in our area, and little by little, people began asking if they could trade or buy from us. Within a year we had enough bread customers to generate the supplemental income needed to meet our modest expenses. And now there is even more demand and a waiting list of neighbors and friends who want our bread regularly. They know our bread is special because the organic wheat is freshly hand milled, the loaves are lovingly made entirely by hand and baked in our outdoor clay oven.

While the key to the lifestyle of voluntary simplicity, is "thinking small," many people still believe the opposite is true-"bigger is better." For example, people often tell us we should invest in a commercial bakery and produce more sourdough bread. But in order to expand and make a career out of baking and selling bread, we would have to go into debt to purchase commercial mixers, freezers and large ovens, work longer hours and face the mountain of bureaucratic permits, codes, fees and restrictions. As a result, the simple, authentic handmade artisan bread that our customers love would have to be sacrificed in favor of expanding volume and making more money. Everybody loses but the bankers and the bureaucrats. We would fall right back in the same old trap, getting into debt and sacrificing our freedom and quality of life for a job. This is an example of compounding inefficiency.

The downfall of many people who would like to break the bonds of stress and financial enslavement to the system is their tendency to think too big. But we must realize that this has been programmed into us by the industrial society and loan institutions, all attempting to excite and feed our insatiable desires. Friends, it takes a lot of mindful awareness to break free of all these traps. It also requires an ability to improvise and adapt towards an alternative model. The lifestyle of voluntary simplicity is one option and the resulting benefits are transformational.

The point I'm making is this: many of us can no longer think in terms of having a lifetime career anymore. For whatever reason, things are changing in this country. Outsourcing and cheaper labor costs in other countries will continue to eliminate jobs in the United

States. And though the opportunity still exists to work, we must understand that it may be only temporary. While continuing to work at a job or career one should be wise and set up a plan to survive without steady employment for certain periods of time if necessary.

This could mean storing some supplies, purchasing a piece of property where a small shelter, tent or tipi can be erected if necessary, or getting out of the city and into the country where one can provide food for themselves. My old Grandpa used to say, "all the troubles in this country began when people stopped growing their own food." And he was right. The younglings of this modern age don't even know what real food is, much less how to grow or prepare it! This has to change. (That's another reason we promote sourdough bread baking. It is time to start a "slow-food" movement).

Thinking small is one of the most intelligent and powerful things one can do. Consciously reducing one's life down to the simple basics is the secret to happiness. And it is so easy. What is the solution? This is our advice, especially to young people:

"Don't get in debt, don't think in terms of a career (work at a job for one reason only, to get paid so you can buy a place to live and grow some food), live in a small shelter, unload unnecessary stuff, reduce monthly expenses, extract yourself from the enslavement of modern technological materialism, stay healthy by exercising, eat a simple, wholesome diet, develop some practical skills, practice your art or trade and serve your local community. Teach your children to value true pleasures. Real wealth is perishable: food, health, trees, flowers, herbs, healthy soil, clean water, fresh air, friends and art. Learn to value and appreciate these above all else."

Of course we realize that everyone has to creatively work out their own unique plan according to their particular circumstances, especially if there are children to raise. (We have six grown children.) But with "small thinking," so many opportunities open up and the more one can release, the more freedom there is to experience with each passing year.

If someone would have suggested to us ten years ago that there was a way for the two of us to live on much less, build our own little hut, buy our freedom, give up steady employment, work fewer hours, become happy, healthy, debt free, self-reliant, and live fearlessly without health insurance, I would have told them they were crazy. This has been an incredible, radical journey for us, but now we know from first hand experience that with vision, patience, self-discipline and courage, it is possible to create such a reality.

Creative voluntary simplicity expands faster than inflation for those who can do it, rather than waste time and energy thinking too big and chasing after more money to find happiness and security.

38

Three Tons Of Food Per Year

From A 1/10 Acre City Lot

Self-sufficient in the city, A Family Of Four With No Jobs

Jules Dervaes is an urban farmer and a proponent of the urban homesteading movement. Dervaes and his three adult children operate an urban market garden in Pasadena, California as well as other websites and online stores related to self-sufficiency and "adapting in place."

Dervaes has a one-tenth acre lot in Pasadena, California, on which he and his family raise three tons of food per year. This provides 75 percent of their annual food needs and helps them sustain an organic produce business. They also raise bees and compost worms.

Dervaes started experimenting with self-sufficiency while he lived in New Zealand and later in Florida, then decided to see how efficient he could make an urban homestead in Pasadena, California, USA. According to Natural Home magazine, *"The Dervaeses' operation is about 60 to 150 times as efficient as their industrial competitors, without relying on chemical fertilizers and pesticides."*

In addition to growing a significant amount of food, the Derveas family attempts to live off-grid as far as possible and have invested significant amounts of money to experiment with other ways of attaining self-sufficiency. They have 12 solar panels on the roof of the house, a biodiesel filling station in the garage, and a solar oven in the backyard; they use a wastewater reclamation system, a dual-

For the time being, if you actually want to develop such ideal asrama, we must have sufficient land, and all other things will gradually grow. For raising crops from the land, how many men will be required—that we must estimate and for herding the cows and feeding them. We must have sufficient pasturing ground to feed the animals all round. We have to maintain the animals throughout their life. We must not make any program for selling them to the slaughterhouses. That is the way of cow protection. Krishna by His practical example taught us to give all protection to the cows and that should be the main business of New Vrindaban. Vrindaban is also known as Gokula. Go means cows, and kula means congregation. Therefore the special feature of New Vrindaban will be cow protection, and by doing so, we shall not be loser. In India of course, a cow is protected and the cowherdsmen they derive sufficient profit by such protection. Cow dung is used as fuel. Cow dung dried in the sunshine kept in stock for utilizing them as fuel in the villages. They get wheat and other cereals produced from the field. There is milk and vegetables and the fuel is cow dung, and thus, they are self-independent in every village. There are hand weavers for the cloth. And the country oil-mill (consisting of a bull walking in circle round two big grinding stones, attached with yoke) grinds the oil seeds into oil. The whole idea is that people residing in New Vrindaban may not have to search out work outside. Arrangements should be such that the residents should be self-satisfied. That will make an ideal asrama. I do not know these ideals can be given practical shape, but I think like that; that people may be happy in any place with land and cow without endeavoring for so-called amenities of modern life—which simply increase anxieties for maintenance and proper equipment. The less we are anxious for maintaining our body and soul together, the more we become favorable for advancing in Krishna Consciousness.

~ Srila Prabhupada (Letter to: Hayagriva, Montreal 14 June, 1968)

flush toilet, a composting toilet, and a number of hand-cranked kitchen appliances (to reduce power consumption). They also use solar drying, and have a cob oven.

Dervaes owns several websites, including julesdervaes. com, pathtofreedom. com, urbanhomestead.org, urbanhomesteading.com, freedomgardens.org, peddlrswagon.com, backyardchickens. org, barnyardsandbackyards.org, thehiddenyears.org, and dervaesinstitute.org. As of 2008, Path to Freedom got five million hits per month from over 125 different countries.

The Dervaes family was featured on National Geographic Channel's Doomsday Preppers in 2012 and briefly appeared in a trailer for the show.

39

Economics

Simple And Natural

By Srila Prabhupada

Money is required for purchasing food, but the animals, they do not know that food can be purchased. They are searching after food. But we are civilized; we are searching after money. Money is required for purchasing food. Why don't you produce food directly? That is intelligence. You are getting money, very good. What is that money? A paper. You are being cheated. It is written there, "hundred dollars." But what is that hundred dollars? It is cheap of..., piece of paper only. But because we are so fool, we

The gigantic industrial enterprises are products of a godless civilization. Godless civilization, they no more can depend on the natural gifts. They think by industrial enterprises, they will get more money and they'll be happy. And to remain satisfied with the food grains, vegetables and natural gifts, that is primitive idea. They say, "It is primitive." When men were not civilized, they would depend on nature, but when they are advanced in civilization, they must discover industrial enterprises.

They do not know what is spiritual life, what is ultimate goal. Simply like cats and dogs. The dog jumps over with four legs, and if a man can jump over with four wheels, then that is advancement. Just see.

~ Srila Prabhupada (Lecture, Srimad-Bhagavatam, Mayapura, October 20, 1974)

are accepting a piece of paper, hundred dollars, and the struggle for existence for a piece of paper. Why don't you be intelligent — "Why shall I take the piece of paper? Give me food"? But that intelligence you have lost. Therefore my Guru Maharaja used to say the present human society is combination of cheaters and cheated, that's all. No intelligent person. Formerly money was gold and silver coins. It had some value. But what is the present currency? Simply piece of paper. Bunch of papers. During the last war the government failed in Germany, and these bunch of papers were thrown in the street. Nobody was caring. Nobody was caring.

So our civilization is based on that way. You require food. That's fact. Therefore Krsna says, *annad bhavanti bhutani* [Bg. 3.14]. You produce your food. Anywhere you can produce your food. There is enough land. In Australia you have got enough land. In Africa you have enough land, uncultivated. No. They'll not produce food. They will produce coffee and tea and slaughter animals. This is their business. I understand that in your country animals are slaughtered and exported for trade. Why export? You produce your own food and be satisfied. Why you are after that piece of hundred dollars paper? Produce your own food and eat sumptuously, be healthy and chant Hare Krsna. This is civilization. This is civilization.

(Lecture, Bhagavad-gita 9.4 — Melbourne, April 22, 1976)

THE AUTHOR

Dr. Sahadeva dasa (Sanjay Shah) is a monk in vaisnava tradition. His areas of work include research in Vedic and contemporary thought, Corporate and educational training, social work and counselling, travelling, writing books and of course, practicing spiritual life and spreading awareness about the same.

He is also an accomplished musician, composer, singer, instruments player and sound engineer. He has more than a dozen albums to his credit so far. (SoulMelodies.com)

His varied interests include alternative holistic living, Vedic studies, social criticism, environment, linguistics, history, art & crafts, nature studies, web technologies etc.

Many of his books have been acclaimed internationally and translated in other languages.

By The Same Author

Oil-Final Countdown To A Global Crisis And Its Solutions
End of Modern Civilization And Alternative Future
To Kill Cow Means To End Human Civilization
Cow And Humanity - Made For Each Other
Cows Are Cool - Love 'Em!
Let's Be Friends - A Curious, Calm Cow
Wondrous Glories of Vraja
We Feel Just Like You Do
*Tsunami Of Diseases Headed Our Way - Know Your Food Before Time
   Runs Out*
*Cow Killing And Beef Export - The Master Plan To Turn India Into A
   Desert*
*Capitalism Communism And Cowism - A New Economics For The 21st `
   Century*
Noble Cow - Munching Grass, Looking Curious And Just Hanging Around
World - Through The Eyes Of Scriptures
To Save Time Is To Lengthen Life
Life Is Nothing But Time - Time Is Life, Life Is Time
Lost Time Is Never Found Again
Spare Us Some Carcasses - An Appeal From The Vultures
An Inch of Time Can Not Be Bought With A Mile of Gold
Cow Dung For Food Security And Survival of Human Race
*Cow Dung – A Down To Earth Solution To Global Warming And
   Climate Change*
*Career Women - The Violence of Modern Jobs And The Lost Art of Home
   Making*
Working Moms And Rise of A Lost Generation
Glories of Thy Wondrous Name
*India A World Leader in Cow Killing And Beef Export - An Italian Did
   It In 10 Years*
As Long As There Are Slaughterhouses, There Will Be Wars
Peak Soil – Industrial Civilization, On The Verge of Eating Itself
If Violence Must Stop, Slaughterhouses Must Close Down
(More information on availability on DrDasa.com)

* 9 7 8 9 3 8 2 9 4 7 2 0 2 *